GHASTLY TRUE TALES OF
THE NORFOLK POISONERS

GHASTLY TRUE TALES OF
The Norfolk Poisoners

PAMELA BROOKS

HALSGROVE

First published in this edition in Great Britain by Halsgrove, 2007

Copyright © 2007 Pamela Brooks

British Library Cataloguing-in-Publication Data
A CIP record for this title is available from the British Library

ISBN 978 1 84114 583 9

HALSGROVE

Halsgrove House
Ryelands Farm Industrial Estate, Bagley Green,
Wellington, Somerset TA21 9PZ
Tel: 01823 653777
Fax: 01823 665294
email: sales@halsgrove.com
website: www.halsgrove.com

Printed and bound by
Cromwell Press, Trowbridge

Contents

Acknowledgements

As always, I owe a great deal to my husband, Gerard, for looking after our children while I was doing research and writing the book. And to Chris and Chloë, my two small research assistants, who came with me on research trips round various museums and locations for photographs.

Thanks also to the staff of Norfolk County Library – particularly to those at Costessey branch and the Local Heritage section in the Norfolk Millennium Library, who were incredibly helpful in giving me access to the books and documents I needed, and to Clare Agate, for help with photographs. And thanks to Victoria Allen for the loan of poison bottles.

Introduction

Poison as an instrument of murder has a very long tradition: from Medea in Greek mythology trying to trick her husband Aegeus into killing his son Theseus with poisoned wine, through to the Roman emperor Nero getting rid of unwanted family members, through to the Borgia family in fifteenth-century Italy.

In Britain, the heyday of the poisoner was the nineteenth century. Particularly before the Arsenic Act of 1851, it was relatively easy to buy poison from chemists and hardware shops, usually with the excuse that it was needed for ridding a house of mice or rats. Or there was Fowler's Solution – a patent medicine used from the early nineteenth century to treat skin disorders, as a painkiller (for neuralgia and lumbago), and even syphilis – which was a mixture of potassium arsenite and lavender water. A single dose of 0.5ml contained 5g of arsenic.

Arsenic was also used in flypapers, and as a pigment in everything from wallpaper to material to sugar decorations – especially green (Scheele's green and emerald green) and yellow (Naples yellow). The pigment Scheele's green was copper arsenite, and was often used in the mid 1800s as a dye for dress fabric. There are plenty of stories of women becoming ill from wearing dresses in a hot room, when the arsenic leached out of the dye and into their skin. There are also plenty of stories about people becoming ill in rooms decorated with green wallpaper, because the fungi living on the wallpaper paste converted the arsenic into a deadly gas, trimethylarsine – known as 'Gosio's gas' after the Italian chemist who discovered it. The medical journal the *Lancet* actually ran a campaign urging manufacturers to ban the use of arsenical green pigments. Red pigments were also a problem, as vermilion had a mercury base.

Administering the poison was easy, too – particularly with white arsenic (also known as arsenic trioxide), which doesn't have a scent or taste. The poison could be mixed into food so the victim would eat it without knowing – although many of the victims of arsenic poisoning soon discovered a 'hot taste' in the food and drink. Usually when it was much too late for the doctors to help.

The symptoms of arsenic poison in particular often mimicked those of common diseases such as cholera and gastroenteritis, so doctors often misdiagnosed it – in the Happisburgh poisonings in the 1830s and 1840s, the causes of death were put down to cholera, old age and – really surprisingly, to modern eyes – a sore throat.

Detection of the murder was difficult, too. For a start, there had to be proof that the death of the victim was due to poison; toxicology was still in its infancy and chemical tests weren't reliable until at least the mid 1830s. (In fact, there wasn't a reliable chemical test for strychnine until the 1860s; in the Palmer poisoning case, 1856, one of the expert witnesses used a frog to prove the presence of strychnine.)

If it was agreed that poison was the cause of death, the coroner or judge would then have to prove that the accused had actually administered the poison.

On top of this, of course, there had to be a motive and 'malice aforethought' on behalf of the poisoner. Sometimes the motive was pure greed – the nineteenth century was also the time when the business of life insurance grew rapidly and, because murder by poison was hard to detect, the life insurance companies couldn't prove fraud and had to pay up. One of the most famous examples of this was in Liverpool in 1884, where the jury discovered that Catherine Flanagan and Margaret Higgins insured the life of Margaret's husband and poisoned him with arsenic; at the trial, it was shown that the pair had insured the lives of relatives, friends and lodgers and then poisoned them so they could claim the insurance. (This – together with the string of poisonings committed by William Palmer, the Rugely poisoner – was one of the reasons why the concept of 'insurable interest' was introduced to life insurance, meaning that you could only insure somebody else's life if you had a financial interest in them remaining alive, i.e. you were a dependant such as a spouse or child.)

Sometimes the motive was jealousy or love triangles – such as the Burnham poisoners in 1835 and Charles Daines in 1839. Murder could sometimes seem the only way out of an unhappy marriage, because divorce was difficult to obtain in the nineteenth century. Before the Matrimonial Causes Act 1857, anyone petitioning for divorce had to claim damages from the adulterer in the civil courts, prove 'matrimonial offence' in the ecclesiastical court, and then go to Parliament for a private Act to settle the property aspects. The cost and complexity of divorce proceedings, as well as the social stigma, meant there were very few divorces; between 1715 and 1852 there were fewer than 250 divorces overall in the country. The Matrimonial Causes Act 1857 allowed the petitioner to sue for divorce in a special section of the High Court, and the divorce rate then rose to about 200 a year. However, the situation still wasn't completely equal before the law: although a man could divorce his wife for adultery, a woman had to prove cruelty as well as adultery before a divorce was granted. Plus there wasn't such a thing as legal aid: the cost of going to court was often way beyond the means of the poorer classes. And, before the Married Women's Property Act was passed in 1882, any money or property a woman had before her marriage immediately belonged to her husband after the marriage – as did her earnings – so a woman trapped in an unhappy marriage with a violent husband, who had no recourse to the law and no money of her own to help her leave her husband and live an independent life elsewhere, could be tempted to take the law into her own hands.

Sometimes the motive was tragic: for example, unmarried mothers, deserted wives or women who had several children and simply didn't have enough food to go round or were likely to be forced into the workhouse would poison their children with an overdose of laudanum rather than watch them starve outside the workhouse or be parted from them in the workhouse . This was particularly true during the 'hungry forties', when failed harvests and rocketing grain prices meant that unemployment and poverty rose sharply. Or, as in the case of Samuel Howlett in 1844, the use of poison could be an attempt to induce a miscarriage that went very badly wrong. Before 1861 abortion was a serious criminal act; abortions carried out after the 'quickening' (when the mother first noticed the baby moving) were punishable by death, and abortions carried out before this point carried a lesser sentence. From 1861, under the Offences Against The Person Act, carrying out an abortion could be punished by imprisonment of at least three years up to life imprisonment, even when performed for medical reasons.

In January 1841, *The Times* published the findings of the *Third Annual Report of the Register of Births, Deaths and Marriages in England and Wales*, saying that 500–600 people were 'ascertained to die by poison every year in England; besides the cases of poisoning which are never detected'. Of these cases, around 20 per cent were ascribed to arsenic poisoning; as *The Times* commented, arsenic is fatal in small quantities, can be mixed with food so there is no taste, and can be 'obtained with almost as much facility as sugar'. The usual reason given for the purchase of arsenic was to kill rats; William Farr, the head of the General Register Office statistics department, commented acerbically, 'It is questionable whether arsenic kills more rats than human beings.'

The Times called for some kind of regulation of poisons; after it was set up in 1842, the Pharmaceutical Society joined in the campaign for regulating poison. A Bill for the Sale of Poisons had been suggested in 1819, but the Committee of Associated Apothecaries opposed it because they said it would 'embarrass the dispensing of medicines'. Jacob Bell, the MP for St Albans (and the son of a Quaker pharmacist who was a founder member of the Pharmaceutical Society), campaigned for a Pharmacy Act regulating the sale of poisons and medications.

An interim measure was the regulation of the sale of poisons in 1851 under the Arsenic Act. This meant that all chemists and hardware shops had to keep a 'poison book'; whenever anyone bought arsenic, both the buyer and the seller had to sign the book, and the purchaser had to be over the age of 21. Arsenic that wasn't used in medicine (or was sold in a quantity of less than 10 lbs) was coloured with soot or indigo so it couldn't be confused with other white powders such as baking powder (as in the case of the Daveys in 1869), salt or sugar. The buyer also had to be known to the seller – and, if not, the buyer had to have a witness who knew both of them and would also sign the register.

There was a late addendum to the Act while it was in the committee stage, due to the case of 'Sally Arsenic'. Sarah Chesham from Clavering in Essex poisoned her sons with arsenic, but the prosecution couldn't prove how she did it so she was acquitted. However, when her husband died in 1850 the authorities were suspicious and arrested her; arsenic was found mixed with rice in her house as well as in the contents of her husband's stomach. She claimed that the arsenic her husband had ingested was part of his medication – which was often true of Victorian medicines; however, her neighbour Hannah Phillips testified that 'Sally Arsenic' had told her how to get rid of her violent husband, by baking a pie of liver and lights, and Sarah Chesham would give her a special seasoning of poison for it. Sarah was found guilty of administering poison with intent and hanged; and the Sale of Arsenic Bill (later the Arsenic Act) had the addition that only adult males could buy arsenic. However the gender restriction clause wasn't part of the final Act: the sale of arsenic was limited by the age of the buyer rather than the gender.

The Arsenic Act 1851 was the first legal restriction on the sale of poison; it was a good start, but there was still a very long way to go.

Firstly, it only applied to arsenic, and other poisons were used. (Admittedly, arsenic was the most commonly used poison – ten out of the sixteen cases in this book involve arsenic; two involve preparations of mercury, two involve strychnine and/or *nux vomica*, one involves opium and one involves phosphorus.) Secondly, as there was no legal definition of a pharmacist, there was no restriction on who could sell the poison, as long as they kept records; all the purchaser had to do was sign the 'poison book' to state how much they'd bought, and no questions were asked until there had been several deaths in mysterious circumstances.

The Times in January 1852 reported, 'Deaths by poison are above the average, and call for a greater vigilance on the part of their vendors, the chymists [sic] and druggists. It is painful to find that in London 28 persons died of poison in 13 weeks.' However this is rather unfair, as pharmacies weren't the only places to sell arsenic; you could also buy it from the grocer's shop, hardware stores and even the village pub. And arsenic was also available in many industries; it was easy for some to go missing.

Even after the Act, deaths by arsenic continued to occur. There were no regulations about how arsenic should be used; in Surrey, 340 children were poisoned in 1857 after drinking milk mixed with water from a boiler that had been descaled, the previous night, using a solution of arsenic.

It took a seriously nasty accident in Bradford in October 1858 – where twenty people died and around two hundred became seriously ill from arsenic poisoning – before regulations were tightened. The Bradford incident occurred when William Hardaker (known as 'Humbug Billy') bought some peppermint sweets from a wholesale confectioner for his market stall. Sugar, the main constituent of lozenges, was expensive, so manufacturers tended to adulterate the sugar with 'daft' or 'daff'– usually substances that looked like sugar and would bulk it out, such as plaster of Paris, powdered limestone or sulphate of lime. In the Bradford case, the wholesaler's lodger was meant to buy some 'daft' from a chemist five miles away in Baildon Bridge – but the chemist himself was ill and his assistant weighed out 12lbs of a white powder he thought was 'daft'… but was actually arsenic trioxide.

The wholesaler's sweetmaker thought that this particular batch of peppermint lozenges looked unusual, and Humbug Billy was ill when he tasted one; but, instead of refusing to buy the sweets, he negotiated a discount because of their odd appearance. He sold his sweets as usual in the market, but then people started to become ill and die. The first two cases – young children – were thought to be due to cholera, but upon investigation it was discovered they bought sweets from Humbug Billy, as did many of the other sick or dying people. The trail was traced backwards, and the wholesaler, the chemist and his assistant were committed for trial on a charge of manslaughter.

In 1868, the Pharmacy Act was passed, which set up a register of people qualified to sell, make and dispense poisons. The Pharmaceutical Society was in charge of the register, and registered sellers of poison had to keep records and obtain the purchaser's signature at the point of sale. This made it much more difficult for potential poisoners, because the purchase could be traced much more easily; the check certainly worked to some degree, because deaths from poisoning in the last third of the century were much lower than in the 1840s and 1850s.

Meanwhile, toxicologists were developing chemical tests to detect poison. The earliest tests involved bubbling hydrogen sulphide gas through a solution containing arsenic; this would produce a yellow precipitate known as orpiment (otherwise known as arsenic sulphide, As_2S_3). However, if the solution was left for a few days, it could lose its colour and juries would refuse to accept it as evidence of the presence of arsenic – as happened in the case of John Bodle in 1832, who murdered his 80-year-old grandfather in Plumstead so he could get a large inheritance. (In France, arsenic was known as *poudre de succession* or 'inheritance powder'.) The jury acquitted Bodle but James Marsh, the chemist who'd presented the evidence to the court, was proved right ten years later: Bodle was convicted of fraud, and then confessed to the murder because he knew he couldn't be tried a second time for the same crime.

The frustration of not being able to convince the jury of what he knew for a fact spurred Marsh into establishing a test for the presence of arsenic that would provide undisputable proof and could be exhibited in court. Finally he established a test in 1836 where the sample of bodily remains were mixed with a strong acid (usually hydrochloric) to destroy all the organic matter and turn the arsenic into a solution form. This solution was then mixed with arsenic-free zinc. If arsenic was present in the sample, it would turn into its gaseous form, arsine (AsH_3) – and when the arsine was passed through a heated tube, it split into hydrogen gas and metallic arsenic. The arsenic formed a black mirror-like film on the cool section of the tube. If the chemist heated the mirror-like film in air, it would convert to white arsenic (arsenic trioxide).

The Marsh test hit the headlines in 1840 during the trial of Marie Lafarge, who killed her blacksmith husband Charles by administering arsenic to him in a slice of cake. However, the test only worked in the laboratory; it wasn't until 1842 that Egar Hugo Reinsch developed a test that could be used on the spot, where a strip of brightly polished copper foil was dipped into the suspect liquid and any arsenic present would be deposited onto the copper. (It also worked for antimony and mercury – two less commonly used poisons.)

However, before any investigations took place, there had to be grounds for suspicion about the death. The first port of call was the coroner – but inquests weren't cheap (the coroner was paid an amount per inquest and travelling expenses), and the fees came out of the county rates. Local justices of the peace had to approve the payments to the coroner, and often refused to pay the fees unless the cause of death was obviously violent. Because coroners weren't salaried until 1861, the clash between JPs and coroners over the costs of inquests meant that some inquests weren't held when they should have been. For example, in Norfolk in the 1840s magistrates actually sent a note to parishes asking them to make strict enquiries before they held an inquest to keep the costs down. Had one of the earlier deaths of Jonathan Balls' children or grandchildren been investigated, it might have prevented a whole string of murders from taking place, so the penny-pinching definitely backfired.

The coroner had the responsibility of conducting the inquest, examining the witnesses and noting down evidence, and then summing up for the jury. Inquests were held in public buildings – often the local pub – and the coroner and jury would view the body of the deceased at the start of the inquest. If enough facts were established to make a trial possible, the case would go to the Assizes and be tried in front of the judge and jury.

It's sometimes said that arsenic was the woman's murder weapon of choice, and certainly some of the most famous arsenic murderers in the nineteenth century were women. Madeleine Smith became notorious in Glasgow in 1857 when she killed her lover with cocoa laced with arsenic – but the jury gave a verdict of 'not proven' because she could have bought the arsenic for cosmetic reasons (some women used arsenic to improve their complexions) or her lover could have been a secret opium-eater. Mary Ann Cotton is thought to have killed at least twenty people – her mother, three husbands, eight of her own children and seven stepchildren – by administering arsenic in cups of tea; she was hanged at Durham jail in March 1873. And in 1889 Florence Maybrick was sentenced to death in Liverpool for administering poison to her husband James by soaking the arsenic out of flypaper and feeding the extracts to him within meat juices and invalid meals. (The sentence was later commuted to life imprisonment; she served 15 years and then returned to America where she died in 1941, aged 79.)

Arsenic caused severe stomach pains and cramp; symptoms of arsenic poisoning also included vomiting and diarrhoea, so Victorian doctors often misdiagnosed arsenic poisoning as gastric fever or dysentery. It could also be misdiagnosed as cholera (as in the case of Mary Wright's husband in 1833), because if someone was given large dose of arsenic their skin would become cold and clammy and their blood pressure would drop rapidly to give a weak, rapid and irregular pulse – symptoms which were also common to cholera.

The best way of detecting arsenic poisoning was when it was already too late – at a post mortem analysis, when the membrane lining the stomach would look badly inflamed and ulcerated.

However, arsenic wasn't the only poison used for murder in the nineteenth century; other substances include *nux vomica* (whose active component is strychnine), ergot, oxalic acid, opium (often in the form of laudanum), antimony (usually in the form of antimony potassium tartrate, more commonly known as tartar emetic), phosphorus, mercuric chloride (better known as corrosive sublimate) and thallium.

There wasn't a reliable test for strychnine until the late nineteenth century, so Dr William Palmer was able to use it to poison more than ten people in Rugely in the mid-nineteenth century, and Thomas Wainewright (a former friend of Dickens and Blake) was thought to have used it in the 1820s and 1830s. However, there wasn't sufficient evidence to arraign Wainewright and he was sentenced to transportation for the insurance fraud rather than for the murder of his sister-in-law.

The Jacobean dramatist John Fletcher called poison the 'coward's weapon'. But in the nineteenth century it hit the headlines and was a very fashionable crime. Although the following cases all took place in Norfolk, they were very much products of their time and their equivalents are found across the country. As detection methods have improved and poison has become more difficult to buy, poisoning has become a much less popular murder weapon; however, after reading these cases, you might never look at a slice of cake in the same way again…

Opinion and Fact:
JAMES MAXEY, 1813

The case of James Maxey was typical of the early nineteenth century: a victim was poisoned and plenty of people suspected the identity of the murderer, but there just wasn't enough evidence to prove a link between suspicion and fact. In the earliest part of the nineteenth century, there weren't reliable tests for every type of poison; as in this case, the surgeons who did a post-mortem on a body could say that a poison was involved, but couldn't prove which one it was.

On 3 August 1813, James Maxey from the village of Hainford, just outside Norwich, was indicted for poisoning his wife and her daughter by a former husband.

The first witness was Mr Chandler, the surgeon at the nearby village of St Faith's, who deposed that on Wednesday 20 May he went to the Maxeys' house and found James's wife Dinah Maxey and her daughter Elizabeth Smith 'labouring under the most excruciating pain with violent retching' and, in spite of medicine, their symptoms grew worse. At 4 p.m., Elizabeth died. Dinah said to Chandler, 'I am certainly poisoned and dying.' He asked her if she knew who did it, but she simply said, 'I will accuse nobody,' and died at midnight.

Chandler did a post-mortem on the bodies the following day, and said that they'd obviously died from poison but he couldn't say exactly what. He said it was probably a mineral poison, which 'produced a greater degree of inflammation' on

Hainford church where Mrs Maxey was buried.

the tissues of the body. He added that it had a 'strong astringent taste', but he didn't think that it was 'nauseous'. And if it had been administered in strong tea – which itself had a strong astringent taste – the taste of the poison could have been masked.

The *Norfolk Chronicle and Norwich Gazette* reported that at the trial, Mr Futter, Elizabeth's 'sweetheart', said that he'd visited Mrs Maxey and Elizabeth on the evening of Tuesday 19 May. They'd had tea together; the water used to make the tea was poured from the kettle that was shown in court as evidence. He and Elizabeth both drank two cups of tea, but Mrs Maxey didn't drink any. Mr Maxey came home at 9 p.m., sat in the chair for half an hour, and then went to bed.

Martha Yems, Dinah's sister, asked Maxey if he was first up in the house in the morning. He said that yes, it was his habit; when he went to work, he shut the door but didn't fasten it. The morning in question, he saw a couple of men near his premises, who told him it was 5 a.m.

An hour and a half later, their neighbour Elizabeth Furness called in on her way to work, when Dinah and her daughter were about to start breakfast. Dinah poured the tea and commented how white the water was; Mrs Furness said it looked as if the kettle had been filled from a milky jug. However, she didn't actually see Dinah or Elizabeth drink the tea.

A few minutes later, neighbour Ann Futter was on her way to work when she heard Dinah calling out in distress. She stopped at the house and discovered that Dinah was ill; within a quarter of an hour, Elizabeth was equally afflicted.

Sarah Steward, another neighbour, went to see Dinah and Elizabeth on Wednesday morning and made some 'peppermint water' for them. She took the water out of the same kettle they'd used to make the breakfast tea. She tasted it before she gave it to them and told the court that her stomach 'in a few minutes was fit to fly open' and she 'could not get about for nearly a month' afterwards. Clearly the poison had been placed in the water in the kettle – and the surgeon added that when he saw the kettle, it 'seemed washed'.

Was it because someone was trying to be helpful and boil water from an untainted source to make Dinah Maxey a comforting drink – or was it because the murderer was trying to cover his or her tracks by removing the evidence of poisoned water? It's a question that wasn't actually raised by the court.

Meanwhile, Martha had heard that her sister and niece were ill. She went to see them; according to the trial report in the *Norfolk Chronicle and*

Norwich Gazette, she found them 'in a bad state'.

Dinah Maxey said, 'Oh, my dear sister, I am poisoned, I am dying; I am poisoned with something that was put into the teakettle; it appeared white.'

Martha, clearly shocked, asked, 'Who did it?'

Dinah replied, 'I think my husband; it cannot be any body [sic] else, because no one has been here but ourselves.' The Maxeys' cottage was one of four tenements under the same roof, according to the witness Mr Futter; the four cottages formed an octagon, and there was a common passage through the middle of the octagon. James Maxey clearly wasn't the only one with an opportunity to drop poison into the kettle, but Dinah Maxey didn't believe any of her neighbours had come in to her house and secretly poisoned her.

Elizabeth died that afternoon while Martha was still there. According to the trial report in *The Times*, James 'came up, making a sad lamentation to think the girl was dead.' Dinah gave him short shrift: 'James, what do you make that piece of work for, when you know you did it to us?' He didn't reply. Dinah wouldn't let him off the hook: 'If you meant to do it to me, you did not want to do it to my child.'

The following day, Ann Futter called in to see how her neighbour was doing. Dinah's response was that she'd been poisoned. Dinah died later that day.

Rumours started to run round the village. Had James Maxey poisoned his wife and stepdaughter? James was either steadfast in his innocence or completely brazen, because he stayed put.

Some of the neighbours even asked him about it. On the day Dinah died, James Cook, a farmer at Hainford, said to Maxey, 'I heard your wife accused you of poisoning her.'

Maxey said, 'She did not agotch [hesitate] to tell me to my face.'

'I hope it isn't true,' Cook said.

Maxey's response: 'I am innocent.'

Two days later Henry Abbot, another farmer at Hainford, asked Maxey if his wife had accused him of murder. This time, Maxey wasn't quite as open as he'd been with Cook. 'No, she didn't.' Abbot didn't think Maxey was guilty, but felt it was his 'duty as a neighbour to ask him on the subject'. However, he added that Maxey hadn't been trying to find out who *did* poison his wife and stepdaughter. And surely the action of an innocent man would be to start asking questions and finding out who might have done the deed?

According to Ann Futter, she'd known the Maxeys for years. 'They lived sometimes well and sometimes ill, just like other people.' She couldn't think of a reason for James to want to murder Dinah.

Ann Futter and Martha Yems were in the cottage on Friday morning (at the incredibly early hour of four in the morning), washing the bedlinen ready to lay the body out. Martha showed Ann 'some white stuff in a paper, which had been found in a little drawer'. Was this the poison used to kill Dinah and Elizabeth?

Martha said she'd found the poison in an unlocked drawer where her sister kept her linen caps. After she'd shown the package to Ann Futter, she'd left the package on the shelf over the fireplace.

So what was the powder?

James Remington, a blacksmith and farrier at Hainford, was Maxey's employer. At the trial, he testified that he'd bought corrosive sublimate 'to cure a horse's foot'.

Corrosive sublimate is better known as mercuric chloride; one of the most notorious cases where this particular poison was used is that of the Marquise de Brinvilliers, who used it to kill her father and two brothers (as well as testing it on several people whom she was meant to be visiting and offering charity). She was found guilty and beheaded in France in 1676.

In the nineteenth century corrosive sublimate was used for making lotions for horses' feet. It was also used as an insecticide, a pesticide and in the treatment of venereal disease. It was a quack cure for other diseases; in 1879, publican William Nixon from Broughton in Lincolnshire, who'd suffered from rheumatism for four of five years and was desperate to stop the pain, was told by a travelling blacksmith that corrosive sublimate could help. Nixon dissolved a piece the size of a pea in a cup of water and drank it – and soon showed signs of being poisoned. The local doctor, Walter Paterson, was called and 'administered an antidote', but it was too late; he died within two days. At the inquest, the doctor said that Nixon had taken enough poison to kill three men, but Nixon himself told the doctor he didn't think 'a little bit like that' would hurt him. The coroner's verdict was that 'the deceased took the deadly poison by mistake, and under the belief it would act as a remedy'.

Nothing is mentioned at the trial of Dinah or Elizabeth being ill, so it's unlikely that James Maxey would have put corrosive sublimate in the kettle as a remedy for illness and accidentally overdosed them.

A the trial, James Remington testified that Maxey had worked for him for fifteen years and during that time 'had behaved himself very well'.

Clearly the coroner had some doubts, because he asked if Maxey had 'made improper language at work'.

Remington thought about it. 'Once after shoeing a vicious donkey, he said, "I'll be d—d if I don't do something to be hanged for, before I will shoe dickies."'

The court accepted that Maxey's patience had been tried – he'd probably been kicked by the donkey and was letting off verbal steam (and in dialect, too – although *The Times* reported that Maxey didn't want to shoe 'donkies' [sic], the *Norfolk Chronicle and Norwich Gazette* used the local word, 'dickey'). It wasn't a statement of intention to murder – especially as he hadn't specified what he'd do or to whom, and in that particular era the 'Bloody Code' was still in force, so there were a couple of hundred crimes that could have resulted in him being hanged. (However, it's also worth noting that those crimes boiled down to about sixteen categories – for example, burning down a cowshed was counted as a separate offence from burning down a stable, but both would fall under the category of arson.)

Remington used corrosive sublimate in his business and had recently purchased an ounce, some of which he'd used and the rest was kept in a cupboard in his workshop. The week after Dinah and Elizabeth died, he'd heard of a cat and dog being poisoned near his shop, so he checked the cupboard and found that a quarter of an ounce was missing. Though he added that Maxey had never asked him for poison.

'Did Maxey know the properties of the poison?' asked the coroner.

Remington's answer: no.

When Maxey was called to the bar, he said that he'd never had any poison and knew nothing about how his wife and stepdaughter had been poisoned.

The judge then explained to the jury about circumstantial evidence and said that 'all links of the chain must be entire and the connection with the guilty party must be obvious and necessary before you could justly and conscientiously give a guilty verdict.'

Clearly the chain wasn't there for Maxey. The evidence they had was that Dinah Maxey and Elizabeth Smith died; at the post-mortem, the doctor said it was due to 'a mineral poison'. A quarter of an ounce of corrosive sublimate (a mineral poison) had gone missing from the workshop of Maxey's employer. A paper containing white powder had been found in a linen drawer in Maxey's 'sleeping quarters'. But there was no evidence to show that Maxey had taken the poison from Remington's workshop; there seemed to be no reason for Maxey wanting to kill his wife and stepdaughter; and crucially the powder found by Dinah's sister wasn't analysed or produced in court.

The judge summed it up for the jury: from the Wednesday evening when Dinah died until the following Monday there were rumours in the village that Maxey had poisoned his wife and stepdaughter, but he didn't try to get away – if he were guilty, surely he would have fled? He'd also he'd slept in the house with dead bodies, which the judge said was 'much in his favour', because if Maxey were guilty his conscience wouldn't have let him do it. He added that the remark about the donkey meant nothing, because Maxey was just irritated by having to deal with a vicious donkey. There was a 'big difference between testimony as fact and testimony as opinion', and on the whole there was not enough evidence to prove his guilt.

The jury acquitted him.

And the truth about who poisoned Dinah and Elizabeth and why is lost to history.

Abominable and Deliberate:
JOHN PYCRAFT, 1819

John Pycraft's case is a strange one. His intended victim was his wife – but it was actually their baby who died. Even though infant mortality was high in the early nineteenth century and parents didn't expect all their children to live, because it was a preventable death we'd expect Pycraft to be upset at losing his infant son (as well as perhaps annoyed that he'd failed to reach his real target, as his wife recovered from the poisoning). Yet, throughout the whole trial, local journalists reported that he was 'unmoved' and showed no remorse for his crimes. Right to the end, Pycraft concentrated on vindicating himself. This didn't endear him to the jury, who were shocked that he'd murdered his own baby.

Pycraft himself made quite a spectacle in court. The trial reports in the *Norfolk and Norwich Chronicle* describe the 35-year-old as 'diminutive and decrepit' – he was only four feet two inches tall – and 'his head was extremely ill-proportioned to his body and limbs, being an unusual size'. He didn't even have the face of an angel to make up for his misshapen body, as they added that he had a 'heavy countenance'. So it's unlikely that Elizabeth Knights married him for his physical attractions. The depositions at the trial make him sound alternately a bully and a whinger, not a man who could turn on the charm – and the attraction wasn't money as he wasn't particularly well off.

Or was he? In the broadside published at his execution (by printer Richard Lane of Bridewell Alley), he's described as a gardener who was paid 6 shillings a week by Squire Peters of Westwick – and Lane adds, 'With which, however, he was enabled by his extreme frugality (being a particular near-living man) to obtain a moderate subsistence and had lately purchased half an acre of land at North Walsham.' So maybe Pycraft wasn't so much poor: he was just very, very careful with his money.

As to his looks: again, Lane counters the reports from the newspapers: 'His countenance exhibited no marks of that ferocious disposition which could stimulate him to the atrocious deed.'

But whatever the reasons behind the Pycrafts' marriage, it clearly wasn't a success. During arguments, both referred to each other's 'damned mother' – and although neighbour Rose Wacey claimed she had no idea that Pycraft didn't get on well with his mother-in-law, her sister Judith Merrison gave more telling evidence under cross-examination. Elizabeth's mother was 'deranged' and had 'been in the Bethel', the hospital built in the centre of Norwich in 1713 by Mary Ann Chapman as a refuge for the mentally ill. Clearly there were tensions between the Pycrafts and the Knights.

Pycraft's hatred for his wife reached a pitch in 1819. The Friday before the Aylsham fair, Pycraft went to see Sarah Spooner, who kept a shop in Worstead. They'd known each other for over twelve years and were on friendly terms; he asked her to bring him a parcel. 'If I could,' she said. And then Pycraft explained that he had rats in his garden – he wanted some poison to get rid of them, and because Sarah was a respectable woman a chemist would give the poison to her. Sarah was clearly not convinced by his argument – although the custom of the time meant that most chemists would insist on a witness being there when the poison was weighed out and given to the customer, there was no reason why Pycraft couldn't get the poison himself.

As for the rats: a witness at the trial said he wasn't aware of rats in Pycraft's garden because they all used traps for vermin. So it seems there was no need for Pycraft to buy arsenic – unless he was planning to use it for other purposes…

On Friday 14 May 1819, Pycraft asked his friend John Spooner to go with him to Norwich. He was still talking about the vermin in his garden and said he wanted to buy threepence-worth of arsenic to kill them. Spooner agreed to go with him to witness the purchase. The female assistant at Purland the chemist's didn't ask their names, but Spooner said at the trial that she weighed out around an ounce of arsenic and wrapped it up in paper. Spooner left the shop with his friend, and they parted company.

Ann Brown, the chemist's assistant, testified that she lived above the shop and had served Pycraft with the arsenic. According to her, the amount was an ounce and a half of arsenic, at a cost of threepence, and she'd wrapped it up 'in two papers'.

On Sunday 16 May, neighbour Rose Wacey saw Elizabeth in the yard with the baby somewhere between five and six p.m. The baby – named John Pycraft, after his father – was nine months old and had been very sickly, but appeared well enough that afternoon.

Shortly afterwards, Pycraft sent for Rose's sister Judith Merrison, whose cottage was about ten yards away on Worstead Lane. Judith came to the Pycrafts' cottage and saw Elizabeth vomiting everywhere. Elizabeth moaned that she was in pain and her throat and stomach felt hot. (These are typical symptoms of arsenic poisoning.) The baby wasn't vomiting but Judith thought he looked a bit red, his eyes were 'started' and his lips were very dry.

A couple of hours later, Pycraft rushed in to Rose, crying, 'Wacey, come in at mine, for my wife and child are dying.' As soon as Rose walked through the door, she saw Elizabeth vomiting copiously. There was some pork on a red saucer on the kitchen table – hardly the sort of food a nine-month-old baby would be given to eat – and a pot of tea. Elizabeth asked for some warm water; Rose gave it to her but it only made Elizabeth sicker. Meanwhile, the baby was on Elizabeth's lap – just as Judith had seen, Rose noticed the baby's lips were parched and dry, his eyes were rolling and he 'moaned very much', although he wasn't actually vomiting. The baby was convulsing; although Rose had never seen the baby have a fit before, she didn't question it.

In the meantime, Pycraft did nothing but sit on a stool next to his wife. Was he paralysed from fear and shock at the reality of what he'd fantasised about? Or was he a cold-blooded murderer who really didn't care that his baby was dying and his wife was seriously ill?

At quarter to ten, Pycraft called for Judith again and said that the child was 'very bad'. Judith took only a couple of minutes to get to the cottage, but it was already too late: the baby was dead. Rose put the child in the cradle, and Judith noted two pieces of bacon on the table in a red saucer, together with some potatoes.

Elizabeth was distraught, yelling at John, 'Damn you, John, you have done for your wife and child, and now you and your damned old mother may do as you like.' John warned her, 'Hold your tongue, Betty, it is only your damned foolishness.' (In court, Judith claimed he added, 'If you do not, I'll kick your damned arse out of doors' – language that must have shocked the jury.)

At this point, Pycraft asked if he should go for the doctor. Elizabeth refused, though a little while later, Pyraft confessed to Rose, 'If my wife requested me to go for the doctor I wouldn't go, I'd go out for a time long enough for me to get to North Walsham, then return and say I'd been for the doctor.'

At midnight, Elizabeth asked Rose to make some tea. Rose took the teapot from the pantry in the next room; when she emptied it, she saw tealeaves sticking inside it. When she asked Elizabeth what was in the teapot, Pycraft cut in hastily, 'Some damned stuff my wife has put in.'

Rose rubbed the white substance between her fingers and said later in court, 'It appeared to waste like pearl-ash in the water.' Meanwhile, Elizabeth was complaining that her throat and stomach felt hot. Arsenic? Perhaps. The symptoms of acute arsenic poisoning usually start with a dry mouth, then nausea and vomiting together with colicky pains and diarrhoea; however, if doses are small and frequent, the symptoms tend to start with flushing of the face and flaking skin on the palms of the hands and soles of the feet, followed by patches of hair loss and swelling in the face, around the eyes and around the ankles.

Rose stayed with Elizabeth until four in the morning, when she said she felt better; then Rose went home.

Some time between six and seven o'clock on the Monday morning, Rose drew some water from the well. Pycraft came over to his old friend in a panic. 'Wacey, if you don't say you eat [sic] some of the pork, I shall be done, for my wife has been telling her damned old mother that the pork was poisoned.'

Later that day, Rose undressed the baby to prepare him for burial. She saw no signs of any swelling in the baby's body. The child was put in the coffin but the top wasn't nailed down. Then she went to see Elizabeth and chatted to her until noon.

By Wednesday 19 May, Pycraft clearly realised what a mess he was in. He told Rose casually that his mother wanted to see her; when she went outside, he went with her and begged for her help. 'Wacey, I am done now if you don't stand my friend, for my wife's old mother has found some more white powder in the teapot.'

'What was it?' Rose asked.

'Poison,' was the laconic reply.

'But how did it get there?'

Pycraft was cool about it. 'I put it in.'

'But – why?' Rose asked.

'To get rid of my wife and child. I could not live with her.'

Rose was shocked but held her peace. She was caught in the worst possible position. If she told the magistrates what Pycraft had told her, he would be hanged. He'd been a friend for years. But if she said nothing – how could she live with herself and the guilt?

Later that day, Pycraft went to see Judith Merrison and told her that his mother-in-law had found more stuff in the teapot; he claimed that his wife 'says I or your sister did it' (which hints that Rose and Elizabeth didn't get on too well). Judith immediately tackled her sister about it, and discovered that Pycraft was lying – no one was accusing Rose of anything.

Pycraft's moods seemed to swing between terror at what he'd done and boastfulness. During the week, he saw Sarah Spooner and told her that he'd killed the baby. Her response was shocked: 'Oh, you cruel man!' She told him immediately to leave her house and never come back.

Elizabeth's brother, William Knights from Scottow, came to see Pycraft later that week. 'I heard you poisoned the child.' Pycraft brazened it out: if it was true, then Knights would have to find out where he'd got the poison. Knights wouldn't find anything because it wasn't true.

Yet his bravado had vanished by Saturday 21 May 1819, when the child's body was to be 'taken up' by the coroner. At ten in the morning, Pycraft went next door to see Rose. 'It's time to go to the church,' he told her. 'The body is to be opened in the church by surgeons.' The magistrate, Mr Cooper, had ordered Rose's sister Judith to be there as well as Pycraft.

'Now I am done,' said Pycraft, 'for the taking up of the child will be a doer for me. I shall go to Norwich Castle and never come back any more.' Again, he told Rose that she had to tell the coroner she'd eaten the pork and drunk the tea. In front of the coroner, Rose duly swore she'd eaten the pork and drank the tea; she said at the trial that she'd given a false account because she was frightened, as she'd already kept the secret for too long.

When the child's body was taken from the coffin, Pycraft confessed his guilt to Judith. But when William Dalrymple, the Norwich surgeon, opened the child's body, he said he couldn't find any evidence of arsenic poisoning. There were some signs but there wasn't enough evidence to stay definitely that the child had been poisoned; he pointed out that other things could have caused the convulsions, such as teething.

The infant John Pycraft was buried on Sunday 22 May. The next day, Pycraft asked Rose to go with him to Captain Cooper in North Walsham. He promised he'd pay her if she swore that Elizabeth put the poison in the teapot herself.

Rose refused.

So at the assizes in August 1819, Pycraft faced three charges. Firstly, that he 'did privately, feloniously and wilfully put a quantity of arsenic into some pork and potatoes prepared for John Pycraft, his infant child', and that his wife Elizabeth had no idea that he'd done this and gave the

The Trial and Execution,
Life, Parentage, & Education,
OF
JOHN PYCRAFT,
AGED 35,

Who was Executed on the Castle Hill, Norwich, on Monday, Aug. 16th, 1819, for the wilful Murder of John Pycraft his infant child.

The above unhappy Criminal is a remarkable and awful instance of the Depravity of human nature, and the fatal effects of not reflecting upon the consequences of giving way to vicious and sinful temptations.—It appears that this miserable man has passed the greatest part of his life in the humble occupation of a Gardener, and was in the employ of Squire Peters of Westwick, where acting as under Gardener he received the small sum of Six Shillings per week, with which however he was enabled by his extreme frugality (being a particular near living man) to obtain a moderate subsistence and has lately purchased half an Acre of land at North Walsham, on which he has built a House; he has been married about two years, during which it seems he has frequently indicated his unhappy disposition in an unnatural dislike to his wife, a quiet and inoffensive woman, with whom he led a very uncomfortable life in consequence of a secret attachment which existed betwixt him and another woman of a bad character. It appears that the object of his diabolical design was not his child, as his intention was evidently to be the death of his wife, and for which purpose, he in company with another man, procured at the Shop of Mr. Purland, Chemist, St. Simon's, an ounce of white Arsenic and afterwards administered the same to his wife, by mixing it with the food which he expected his wife only would partake of, but unfortunately the child became the innocent victim of the fatal drug; but being immediately interred, the cause of its death was not discovered till fourteen days afterwards, when a suspicion arose in the neighbourhood, and on examining the Corpse, (after it had been taken up) the child was found to have been poisoned, and in consequence of certain words which dropped from the father, it was strongly suspected that he was its murderer—the Coroner's Jury which sit on the body, accordingly brought in their Verdict of Wilful Murder against John Pycraft.

His Trial which came on on Friday last, lasted six hours, during which time twenty six witnesses appeared against him, and the circumstances of the murder being clearly made out, the Jury found him GUILTY!—The awful sentence of the Law was immediately passed, that he should be hung by the neck till he was dead, and his body afterwards delivered to the Surgeons for dissection.

He was a man of a very diminutive stature, and an uncommon singular appearance, the length of his body being so disproportioned, and his legs unusually short, still however, his countenance exhibited no marks of that ferocious disposition which could stigmulate him to the atrocious deed; neither does it appear from what we have been able to collect concerning him, that his conduct previous to this murder was ever known to be remarkably bad; nor was he a man by any means addicted to drunkenness, but on the contrary, of a particular sober habit, owing in some measure to his penurious disposition. However he appears to have had a dislike to his wife without any provocation on her part, which so completely divested his mind of every feeling of humanity; that he had for some time thirsted for her blood, in order as it is supposed that he might the more easily follow his vicious inclinations by a connexion with a dissolute woman, in preference of whom he would have made no scruple in sacrificing the life of his lawful wife, and which finally induced him to take away the life of his innocent and unoffending infant, who with its mother look'd to him as their only protection, and who were naturally the objects which ought to have been most dear to him.—What must have been the feelings of such a father when viewing the lifeless corpse of his innocent child murdered by the parent whose delight ought to have been to have cherished it in his bosom! The father who could look without remorse at an unnatural dead was unworthy to live, and was justly punished by an ignominious death.

He was accordingly Executed pursuant to his sentence amidst a vast concourse of spectators who assembled on the Castle Hill at an early hour to witness the awful retribution of Justice; and though amongst them were numbers who lived in the neighbourhood of the culprit and consequently were personally acquainted with him, yet such was the feeling of horror excited by his Guilt, that few were seen to be affected with pity towards him; for disgust at his unnatural conduct took place of the commiseration which otherwise would have been bestowed upon him, and he was launched into eternity an awful and striking example of the dispensation of Providence in bringing to light the deeds of darkness committed by a murderer, which though perhaps impenetrable to human eye, can never be concealed from that Omnipotent Being who "searcheth the hearts of men."

DEATH! 'tis a melancholy day
To those that have no God,
When the poor soul is forc'd away
To seek her last abode.

In vain to heaven she lifts her eyes,
But guilt, a heavy chain,
Still drags her downward from the skies,
To darkness, fire, and pain.

Awake, and mourn, ye heirs of hell,
Let stubborn sinners fear;
You must be driv'n from earth, and dwell,
A long for ever there.

What shall the wretch, the sinner do,
He once defied the Lord;
But he shall dread the Thund'rer now,
And sink beneath his word.

Tempests of anger fire shall roll,
To blast the rebel worm,
And beat upon his naked soul
In one eternal storm.

Prepare me, Lord, for thy right hand,
Then come the joyful day;
Come, death, and some celestial band,
To bear my soul away.

[R. LANE, PRINTER, BRIDEWELL-ALLEY, NORWICH.]

Gallows broadside for John Pycraft. © Norfolk County Council Library and Information Service food to the child, who then ate it and died. Secondly, that he'd put arsenic in tea prepared for the child; and thirdly, that he'd administered poison, with the intent to kill and murder his infant child.

The case was put to the jury in a six-hour trial. Rose said she had no idea the child had even started cutting any teeth, and Judith pointed out that a big piece of fat pork was hardly the sort of food a nine-month-old baby would be given. But under cross-examination they both made damning admissions – particularly Rose, who quoted Pycraft as saying, 'I wouldn't mind being hanged if my wife had died too.'

The medical witnesses, too, were against Pycraft. Both the surgeon William Dalrymple and the chemist William Sharpe testified that if they'd been told the child had been given arsenic at eight o'clock and died at ten, they would have attributed the symptoms they'd found to arsenic poisoning rather than natural causes.

The judge summed up the six-hour case in an hour and five minutes, and the jury took only a few minutes to find him guilty – in their view, even if Pycraft had hated his wife, he should not have taken it out on the child. The judge, Justice Burrough, said, 'In the history of the criminal law of England, a more abominable, more deliberate and more deep-formed design was not to be found.' Then he sentenced Pycraft to hanging and dissection.

Pycraft confessed that he put the arsenic in the tea; he was sitting at home near his wife, and saw her drink the tea and give some to the child. The baby died four hours later but his wife recovered.

His fate was sealed; though clearly he patched things up to some degree with Elizabeth, because she visited him in prison and he gave her money.

Pycraft slept badly, the

Walsham church where Pycraft's son was buried.

27

night before the execution. Then on the morning of Monday 15 August, he took the sacrament at the castle chapel. His arms were pinned and he was marched to the scaffold on Castle Hill. He stood firm while the rope was put round his neck. At 12.15 precisely, the platform fell, and the crowd was treated to more of a spectacle than they'd bargained for. For the next seven to eight minutes, according to the *Norfolk Chronicle,* Pycraft 'was a little convoluted and his chest expanded' but 'apparently without any conscious sensation of pain'.

Maybe the hangman had misjudged the drop. Afterwards, Pycraft's body was taken to the Shire Hall for dissection, his body was exhibited for an hour after dissection – and the local paper took a rather unhealthy interest in detailing every single measurement! – and finally the 'abominable and deliberate' murderer was buried in the castle grounds.

Yarmouth Court's
Last Sentence of Death:
THE NEAL FAMILY, 1825

The case of the Neal family was the last sentence of death issued by the Yarmouth Sessions Court. After then, all cases where the death sentence was a possibility were tried in Norwich.

The case was unusual in that a whole family, rather than just one person, was accused of the attempted murder: so it's quite understandable that a pamphlet about the case calls it a 'Singular Trial'. (The full title of the pamphlet – typical of the early nineteenth century – is incredibly long to modern eyes: *The Singular Trial of Mary Neal, Susan Neal and William Neal for attempting to poison by means of White Arsenic William Hales, his wife and three children, also Elizabeth Fenn their Servant at the general sessions of the peace Yarmouth April 29th 1825.*)

The pamphlet was sold for 6d from the printer's shop in Post Office Row, Great Yarmouth, and an associate in Norwich. Its author, J. Barnes, explains exactly why arsenic was one of the most popular poisons used in murder.

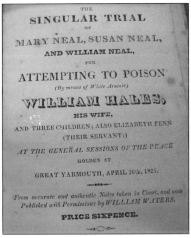

Front page of the pamphlet about the trial, held in the Norfolk Heritage Centre, Norfolk & Norwich Millennium Library. Reproduced with permission of Norfolk County Council Library and Information Service

The Italian writer Morsagni [speaks of] poisoning a very large company at Italian feast by sprinkling desert [sic] with arsenic instead of flour. Arsenic is that of the mineral poisons, which is chiefly employed as the instrument of crime; the

reason probably is, that it is of easy access, requires no prepa-
ration and at the same time as it is so destructive in small
doses, is so little disgusting in flavour, as to furnish the assas-
sin with the sure and secret means of destruction.

In the nineteenth century, there would often be several counts on the indictment to make sure that people weren't acquitted on a technicality due to poor wording by a clerk. In this case, there were six counts. The first was 'feloniously, wilfully, maliciously and unlawfully and of their malice aforethought attempted to poison one William Hales, Maria Hales, Maria Hales the younger, Mary Elizabeth Hales, William Hales the younger and Elizabeth Fenn by mixing one ounce of white arsenic with soup and causing the same to be taken by William Hales and others'. The second was 'causing to be administered to and taken by William Hales, Maria Hales, Maria Hales the younger, Mary Elizabeth Hales, William Hales the younger and Elizabeth Fenn "a certain noxious and destructive substance to poison, kill and murder the same"' – and from there on the counts appear to be substantially the same but the list of victims becomes much shorter.

The lawyers here were taking no chances. If the first indictment had been the only one and it could be proved that the Neals hadn't intended to poison the servant, they could have been acquitted. So the later indict-

Yarmouth Tolhouse where the
Neal family were indicted.

ments cover just Hales, his wife and children; and then just Hales himself, because the lawyers clearly thought that he was the main target.

According to the *Norfolk Chronicle and Norwich Gazette*, the court was 'crowded to excess' on the day of the trial. The details revealed by the trial show just how lax the poison-sellers were; and it's very diffi-cult to say what really did happen. The Hales family appear to have found fault with all their servants, so they were probably very unpleasant to work for. Meanwhile the Neals are described almost as paragons of virtue by their neighbours – but in court Mary Neal tried to shift blame onto her daughter, while Susan tried to shift the blame onto her mother. Clearly they were facing serious charges – charges that could mean a death sentence – and the Neals were terrified that they'd be found guilty: but it seems odd that mother and daughter were prepared to let the other take the blame.

The crux of the matter appears to be William's indenture of apprenticeship. Basically the indenture was a legal document; a master would agree to instruct an apprentice in that trade for a set term of years (usually seven), in exchange for a sum of money (known as a premium). The document set out what the apprentice had to do, including requirements about behaviour (often 'no fornicating', no gambling, and not getting married until the term of apprenticeship ended); and it also set out what the master would do as well as teach the apprentice, which often included giving board and lodging and clothes.

William Neal had been bound as an apprentice to the cordwainer (shoemaker) William Hales in Howard Street two years before, when he was sixteen – which in itself is unusual, as most apprentices were aged between twelve and fourteen when the indenture was signed. Susan Neal agreed to pay Hales twenty shillings (£1) – but then didn't pay him. The row escalated and ended with the Neals in court, charged with an attempt to kill Hales and his family.

The first witness was Philip Gilman Howlet, assistant to Mr Sothern, the chemist and druggist in Gaol Street. His testimony is staggering, because it shows just how casual attitudes were towards dangerous chemicals in the early nineteenth century.

On 26 February 1825 two people came to the shop at around 9 or 10 p.m. and asked Howlet for a pennyworth of arsenic to poison rats and mice. The woman said that she'd brought her daughter as a witness; Howlet asked if she were over 13 (she was actually 21 at the time). The woman said yes, so he went into the warehouse and got her some arsenic, weighing somewhere between half an ounce and an ounce.

At this point, one of the jurors asked if he weighed the arsenic.

Howlet: 'No, never.'

So even if the arsenic was found, without knowing how much exactly was bought there was no way of proving how much had been used.

Clearly the court weren't happy with the way he'd conducted himself because the judge reminded him that he should 'always enter the selling of arsenic in a book'. It wasn't a legal duty until 1851, but it was a practice that most chemists adopted. Howlet clearly hadn't bothered writing it down, or there would have been proof that the Neals bought the arsenic there rather than the farcical questions that ensued.

Howlet did wrap the arsenic in two papers, as was customary, and wrote 'arsenic, poison' on each paper. Then he admitted further reckless-ness with the powder, because he'd told Mary Neal to be careful – while getting the arsenic for her, he'd 'spilt some, blew it off a post and inhaled some'. He was lucky not to be seriously ill!

William Pratt, the Sergeant at Mace, showed Howlet a packet of arsenic which had been found on top of the clock case at the Neals' house. Howlet confirmed it was his handwriting on both papers, and this was the packet he'd given to the people who'd come to the shop on 26 February.

Pratt then examined Mary Neal. Did she have rats or mice?

No, she hadn't seen any.

Did she have any arsenic?

She didn't know what it was. She'd never seen any... and then she remembered her husband had once had some on his ship, but she'd never had any in the house and she'd never bought any at Sothern's. (Her denials at this point sound full of panic.) She knew of the chemists Sothern, Nash, Davie and Sancroft; she'd bought spices at Davie's before.

Susan Neal took the stand next. She didn't know what arsenic was and hadn't seen rats on the premises. She'd never gone to the chemist to buy arsenic... Then she clearly realised that the chemist's assistant would have told the court what he knew, and she admitted she'd bought arsenic about a year ago, before Christmas. Howlet was brought back in, and Susan agreed that she'd bought the arsenic from him. She remembered because 'he'd got some arsenic in his mouth' when she bought it. She'd needed the arsenic to get rid of some mice; she'd spread some on a piece of bread and put it in the back closet, then gave the rest of the poison to her mother.

Mary Neal came back and changed her statement: she'd bought arsenic at Sothern's shop and spread it on bread to poison the mice, but she and her daughter had done it when her sons had gone to bed. Clearly she was trying to protect William, but Susan wasn't so lucky – Mary claimed that she'd give the rest of the poison to her daughter.

William Hales took the stand. He confirmed that he was a cordwainer and William Neal, the 18-year-old son of Mary, was his apprentice. In March, around the time of the poisoning, they'd worked together in the kitchen under the shop; it had been just the two of them. On Tuesday 8 March, there was a 'boiler' in the kitchen which contained the liquor in which the beef had been boiled. He and his family ate the beef that night, with no ill effects, then put the boiler in the kitchen. Around 8 p.m. he'd left William Neal alone in the kitchen, but the boy hadn't been in the kitchen on his own on the Wednesday.

On Wednesday 9 March, William had some broth that was made from the liquor in the boiler; it was heated on the fire in the 'keeping room'. He went up to have his dinner and discovered that his wife and three-year-old child were in the sleeping room in bed, very ill. He, the other two children and Elizabeth Fenn the servant ate dumplings and turnips that had been boiled in the liquor from the boiler; William Neal had gone home to have dinner with his family. After a quarter of an hour, he felt sick and the children and servant were ill. The youngest child was 'violently sick with perspiration'. He sent for Mr Costerton the surgeon; Costerton wasn't there, but his assistant came with Mr Barrett and gave them all some medicine. At this point, William Neal returned to find the household ill.

Then the row about the apprenticeship became very public. Hales complained that he had 'had frequent words with his apprentice' and 'had him up twice before the mayor'. He complained that he'd 'had words' with Mrs Neal two years ago, when they contracted a bill and she agreed that she would buy the indenture of her son; but before William was bound as an apprentice she said her husband was lost at sea and she couldn't pay it.

Mr Hales clearly wasn't all thunder, because he agreed to pay half the cost of the indenture. Mary Neal asked him not to say anything about it because then her sister would pay half – perhaps rather parsimonious on Mary's behalf, but then again as a sailor's widow who was already in debt, she was desperate for all the help she could get. (Rachel Woolsey, a friend of Mary Neal, admitted that Mary called on her just after she'd been summoned for debt to the Court of Conscience on 25 February. She was 'in a state' because she'd 'had the summons and couldn't pay'. Rachel added that Mary sounded in despair when she said she 'supposed Mr Hales would be the next to summon her'.)

Hales testified that he gave Mary Neal the bill for 20 shillings and a credit of 10 shillings for the indenture. She wasn't happy because she 'intended to pay a different way' (what she actually meant here is unclear), and she asked him to alter his book (which could have meant the indenture itself or his records). Hales refused, and Mary 'abused him'. He sent her another bill, the following year, and her response was to 'abuse [him] and said she owed [him] nothing'. Five or six months ago, she abused him in the street and said 'that she could do us an injury if she liked'.

Clearly there was no love lost between them, and Hales admitted that he'd seen her in the street since but ignored her. It sounds as if he took out his frustration on his apprentice, though, as he said he'd 'had words' with his apprentice and 'the boy had conducted himself very unruly'. His wife also had an apprentice in her dressmaking business, Maria Skoyles, who worked in the house but didn't eat there.

Maria Hales took the stand next. She deposed that she had three children, who were respectively three years old, two years old and eleven months old. She had a partner in her business, Elizabeth Bloom, who wasn't at the business on 8 or 9 March. On Wednesday 9 March, the servant Elizabeth Fenn brought the boiler from the kitchen into the tearoom to prepare for dinner. She heated the boiler and Maria tasted the liquor; she and the boy drank and were ill within a quarter of an hour. She was violently sick but brought up nothing; she had a headache and 'an oppression on [her] stomach'. She'd been ill for a week, and hadn't really felt well since.

Then came some very telling evidence: Maria Hales had quarrelled with her husband's apprentice, 'but not lately'. She'd also 'found fault' with Fenn. Maria Skoyles, her own apprentice, deposed that she didn't help make dinner that day and had 'been told off for lateness'.

Were William and Maria Hales unlucky in having feckless apprentices, or were they extremely difficult to work for? What were the chances of them having three apprentices/servants at the same time that they had to keep telling off?

Elizabeth Fenn testified next. She explained that she'd brought the boiler from the kitchen, then added potatoes and thickening and dumplings; she explained that 'thickening' was flour from the baker's. She felt ill before she finished her dinner; she felt sick and had stomach pains, vomited, and was ill the next day.

Charles Costerton, the surgeon, stated that he was sent for at 3 p.m. on 9 March. Hales, his children and the servant were retching, all suffering from a burning pain in their stomach. He saw them again at 6 p.m. and they were worse. The next morning, he came at 8 and they told him they'd had a restless night. At 2 p.m. the children started to improve, but he needed to attend the family for five days.

Costerton explained the symptoms of arsenic poisoning to the jury: the victim would feel a burning heat in their stomach and suffer from tremors, perspiration and sickness, though not always dizziness. The symptoms of the Hales family and Eliza Fenn sounded exactly like those of arsenic poisoning.

It was obvious to him that there would be an investigation, and that the food they'd eaten at dinner was probably poisoned. Clearly there would need to be tests, so he took soup from the boiler and poured into a jug. That evening, he took it to the chemist Mr Davie for analysis.

So far, so good – but his next set of tests would horrify anyone in this century. In the early nineteenth century people were far less sentimental about animals, but it seems incredible now: 'I kept some myself and fed it to a small dog in good health, who was violently sick within 3 minutes.' Costerton was quite sanguine about it; he claimed that 'arsenic administered in broth to dogs is not generally fatal'.

Next was a piece of pure drama: a hot poker was brought into the court, arsenic was sprinkled on it, and the room was filled with the scent of garlic – one of the standard chemical tests of the day.

Cufaude Davey, the chemist from the quayside, came onto the stand and testified that he'd been a chemist for fourteen years and had 'subjected the broth to tests'. The first was mixing it with 'sulphuretted hydrogen gas', which gave the result of a yellow precipitate 'known as orpiment or sulphuret of arsenic'. The second test was 'sulphat [sic] of copper and potash', and again there was a yellow precipitate signifying the presence of arsenic. The final test was 'sulphat [sic] of copper and a solution of ammonia'. This was a colour-change test; Davey deposed that after the mixture had stood for a few hours 'the mazarine blue turned grass green'.

He also heated the mixture and produced solid arsenic.

From the evidence, the Hales family had been given arsenic, via the broth that went with their dumplings. Mary and Susan Neal had bought arsenic from Sothern's chemist – arsenic that had been found on top of the clock case when their house was searched. Although they claimed that the arsenic had been to poison vermin, three neighbours (Mrs Powley, Lydia Brown and Mrs Boulter) testified that there were no rats in the Neal house.

Mary was desperately in debt and couldn't pay the indenture money for her son; and it seemed that William and Maria Hales were constantly 'having words' with their servants and apprentices, who must have had a miserable life. Mary was probably well aware that her son was unhappy, and why. The prosecution's view was that Mary had badgered William into putting the arsenic into his master's food – this would have released William from a miserable apprenticeship and also made sure that Mary wasn't summoned for debt. So there was motive, means and opportunity.

The Neals were brought back into court. Mary and Susan said they were innocent; William said he was innocent and heard his master say he had a very bad-principled girl living with him (meaning Fenn).

Character witnesses stuck up for the Neals. Schoolmaster Robert Brightman said that William had studied with him for three years and had very mild disposition, not revengeful or malicious; Susan had studied with him for a year and a half and was also 'very mild'. Hannah Bowles stated that she'd known Mary Neal for 24 years, and she was a valuable character – not malicious at all. Mary Page of Lee's Row agreed that there was no malice in Mary Neal, and she'd known Mary for 20 years and Susan from infancy. John Collins, painter, said he'd known Mary for 15 years and she was a good neighbour. Francis Bartly deposed that he had known her for 10 years, and she wasn't malicious or revengeful: her daughter had a good disposition, and her son was a good-tempered and inoffensive lad.

The trial lasted for eight hours and the jury returned their verdict in twenty minutes: guilty, but they recommended mercy.

The recorder consulted the mayor and asked why the Neals should not be sentenced to death; no one said anything, so he passed the death sentence. It was the last death sentence passed by the Yarmouth Sessions court, who lost the power to pass the death sentence in 1835.

The following Sunday, William Neal confessed to visiting magistrates of the gaol that he put poison in the boiler. He'd got it from the top of the clock. He said he did it because his master behaved ill to him; he would have told before but was ashamed, and his mother and sister knew nothing about what he'd done.

The sentences were commuted to transportation to Australia for life.

The Dumpling Poisoner:
JOHN STRATFORD, 1829

John Stratford's case is a strange one. Why would a man who was ambitious enough to learn to read and write and move beyond his peasant farming family – becoming a whitesmith and engineer – throw it all away by murdering someone? And why would a man who apparently adored his family risk it all by having an affair with another woman? Was it simply that he'd fallen in love with Jane Briggs and would do anything to be with her?

The local papers blamed it on his reading material – Stratford read 'dangerous pamphlets' and the works of Thomas Paine. Stratford's confession was even odder – he said he put the arsenic in the flour but 'it did not occur to me at the time that I was committing any crime'. He'd grown up tending sheep; as farms always had rodent problems which were dealt with by the use of arsenic or fig powder (*nux vomica*), he must have known perfectly well that giving arsenic to someone would result in death. He said in his confession that his 'object was to destroy Briggs, from the fear that the exposure of my intimacy with the woman Briggs would break the peace between my wife and me' – but Thomas Briggs was in the workhouse. He wouldn't even see Stratford's wife to tell her about the affair; whereas Jane Briggs was friendly with Stratford's wife and her pregnancy would be obvious. Killing Briggs wouldn't keep the situation from Stratford's wife at all, and Stratford was bright enough to know that. So it just doesn't add up.

Stratford's early life has very strong parallels with Thomas Hardy's *Jude the Obscure*: he was born into a peasant farming family, grew up tending sheep and became a blacksmith's apprentice at the age of eleven. He was particularly good at his job, because his work as an apprentice was described as better than the journeymen (qualified) smiths. And he clearly wanted to better himself, because when he sold his apprentices' perks of 'ringings and stumpings' (metal offcuts) to shoemakers, he didn't spend his money in the pub – he bought a spelling book and paper and taught himself to read and write. Because his master wouldn't let him have a candle, Stratford used to go into the churchyard on moonlit

*Postwick church where John Stratford taught
himself to write on moonlit nights.*

nights to use a tombstone as a table when he practised writing.

When his apprenticeship finished, Stratford became a journeyman smith, got married, and moved to Norwich where he worked as a millwright and engineer, building up enough of a business to 'afford a decent subsistence for himself and his equally industrious and more prudent wife', according to the *Norfolk Chronicle*. The paper also described him as being 'a kind and affectionate father' to his six children, and 'decorous and respectful; kind in his behaviour to others', and talked about 'that clear natural sense by which his conversation was so remarkably distinguished'. Nine influential citizens testified at his trial, and all gave him the same reference: in the words of the druggist Charles Cross, 'he always bore a very good character'. Everyone seems to have liked him; he worked hard and cared for his family; he wasn't a social misfit; and he simply doesn't fit the mould of the more violent men indicted in Norwich for murder in the nineteenth century.

Stratford was indicted for murdering John Burgess by arsenic poisoning. He pleaded not guilty, because his target wasn't Burgess – it was Thomas Briggs. Briggs was in the workhouse with cancer of the face and was seriously ill. The Briggs and Stratford families had been friendly for seven years, and they'd never fallen out or had any disagreements. According to Stratford, Jane was distraught about her husband's illness and said, 'What a blessing it would be if God would release him from his sufferings.' So had Stratford planned a mercy killing, to save his friend from suffering?

In court, a different story emerged. Stratford was apparently an attractive man; according to the *Norfolk Chronicle* he was nearly six feet tall, athletic and well proportioned, but 'his legs were unsound' and his feet 'badly shaped even to deformity'. Stratford definitely enjoyed his social life – the *Norfolk Chronicle* reported that as soon as his apprenticeship had finished he dropped his studies in favour of 'the rustic gaieties of the district'. And after he moved to Norwich he had an affair with Jane Briggs.

Local opinion of Jane Briggs wasn't good – one of the broadsides published at his execution refers to her as 'this disgrace to her sex', 'this wanton', and 'the woman who was the original cause of his guilt'. So maybe she instigated the affair. The result was that Jane became pregnant with Stratford's child – after Thomas Briggs went into the workhouse as a pauper. She told Stratford about it just before Christmas, when she was 'two months gone', and claimed in court that 'he said he was sorry for it, and hoped I should not go my time'. She mentioned it to him several times and he 'begged [her] to keep [her] situation as quiet as possible' as he didn't want to 'break the peace between him and his wife'; Jane said she hadn't yet told her husband and Stratford promised her that she 'should not want'. She had the baby in June; but meanwhile Stratford had hatched his murder plans. Jane had told Stratford's wife that she sent her husband flour every week, either by Nurse Burgess or by taking it to the workhouse herself. The flour was used to thicken milk which was 'put into a small tin pot made on purpose'. According to the broadsheet, this 'thickened milk' was the only food that Briggs could tolerate, though Jane backtracked here: 'can't say I have mentioned that to Stratford'.

Three weeks after Jane told him that she was pregnant, in January 1829, Stratford went to the druggist Charles Cross in King Street to buy arsenic. He took Thomas Colman with him as a witness (which Cross said was the usual practice) and bought two ounces of arsenic 'for the purpose of poisoning rats'. Stratford wanted crude arsenic – apparently the strongest – but Cross only had 'powdered', so Stratford bought tuppence-worth and Cross's apprentice measured it for him and wrote 'poison' on the white and brown paper used to wrap the drug. Under cross-examination, Cross added that Stratford also used arsenic in his metal work and had discussed it with him. So there was a good reason for Stratford to buy arsenic in the first place.

Susannah Hook, a twenty-year-old servant at the workhouse who'd been there for two years, said that she'd seen him three times before, and he delivered a brown paper parcel to the workhouse, about three weeks before Burgess' death. He said the parcel was for Mr Briggs and that he didn't need to take it up himself – it would 'do quite as well' for Susannah to take it. She put it on the kitchen windowsill and continued working in the kitchen; an hour later, the workhouse nurse Rhoda Burgess came into the kitchen and Susannah gave the parcel 'in the same state to Mrs Burgess as I took it'.

Rhoda's job was to attend Briggs, so she took the parcel to Briggs, who asked her if there was money in it. Rhoda's husband John Burgess was sitting at the foot of Briggs' bed and opened it to check; he said it was just flour and put the parcel in the cupboard at the foot of Briggs' bed, which Rhoda later said wasn't locked. Briggs didn't use the flour (which seems odd, as it was the only foodstuff he could eat), but after three weeks he suggested that Rhoda Burgess should take it and use it herself, 'as he had no occasion for it, and thought it a pity the flour should be spoiled'.

On Monday 2 March, while Rhoda was out, John Burgess took the flour with the aim of 'making up the flour'. According to Rhoda, her husband was making flour into dumplings; Rhoda knew she had no flour in the house and, although she didn't see John take the flour out of the bag, she recognised the paper containing the flour as that from Briggs' parcel.

Burgess finished cooking the dumplings and cut them up. Rhoda noticed 'a dirty white froth on top of the water' and refused his offer of a piece of dumpling because she thought there was something wrong with it (though it isn't recorded that she tried to stop her husband eating *his* portion!). But when she saw Burgess eating heartily with no apparent ill effects, she gave two pieces of dumpling to her son, ate a piece herself and gave some to other people in the kitchen, then some to Mary Morse and Ann Pillar – presumably colleagues.

Shortly afterwards, Rhoda felt violently sick. Her husband felt 'so bad he went down to get some beer'. Half an hour later, he had to be helped onto the bed. Burgess said he was a dying man and his 'eyesight was leaving him very fast'. He retched but couldn't bring up the dumplings; Rhoda herself was violently sick.

Her son called two of the city surgeons, John Coleman and James Robinson, to help them. Coleman realised straightaway that Burgess was dying – 'the pupils of his eyes were dilated, his body and extremities were cold, pulse hardly perceptible'. Coleman tried to encourage him to drink warm water but Burgess said it was no use because he was dying – he'd been poisoned. He told Coleman that he'd made the dough himself and the bag was in the other room. Coleman took the flour and remaining dough away for testing and attended the post mortem, where he said Burgess' stomach 'had all the appearances as if...[he'd] died from... a mineral poison'. Robinson corroborated the statement.

William Dalrymple, who carried out the post mortem, went into great detail in the trial about the procedure and the signs of arsenic poisoning. The membrane lining Burgess' stomach was highly inflamed with three deeper spots which Dalrymple believed was caused by arsenic. Burgess' heart was full of blood 'in a fluid state' and his lungs and liver were 'gorged with blood'. Dalrymple was absolutely sure that Burgess had 'died of some acrid poison', but was more cautious about saying which poison: he thought it was arsenic. He took about ten ounces of fluid from Burgess' stomach for analysis and gave it to Mr Stark, a Norwich chemist who'd helped with previous post-mortems of poison victims and who 'has attended to experimental chemistry for many years'.

Stark testified about the forensic analysis of the flour and dough. He dried a piece of dough and applied it to a red-hot metal – the result was a 'garlick-like [sic] smell peculiar to arsenic'. He boiled another piece of dough in distilled water and mixed the cooled liquid with three different substances, all of which indicated the presence of arsenic – 'ammoniuret of silver' gave a bright yellow precipitate, 'ammoniuret of copper' gave a grass-green precipitate, and sulphurated hydrogen gave a bright lemon precipitate. Just in case the dumplings had contained salt which might affect the test, Stark tested the liquid with nitric acid, nitrate of silver and liquid ammonia – the resulting yellow liquid indicated the presence of arsenic. But when he tested the flour, there was no sign of any poison. A few days later, Stark tested the stomach contents Dalrymple had given him, first filtering out the 'solid parts'. He applied the same chemicals with similar results (though 'to a less intense degree'). He then made precipitates of the liquid of the dough, dried them and 'subject[ed] them to the process of sublimation' – producing metallic arsenic. A few days later, he 'brushed with a feather a few grains of flour from the inside of the brown paper bag', tested the flour and discovered traces of arsenic.

Thomas Briggs gave his testimony with a veil over his face 'such was its dreadful appearance produced by cancer'. The *Norwich Mercury* added that he needed Mr Robinson the surgeon to act as an interpreter in court, because 'he spoke so as to scarcely make him understood, even by those most accustomed to attend him'. He said that he'd been sent some flour by 'some person' in February but had asked Rhoda to put it in the cupboard until he wanted it. He said told the court, 'I mostly lie in bed with my face covered,' and he hadn't seen John Burgess take the flour. Several witnesses testified that no person had access to Briggs' room; and Jane Briggs told the court that her husband knew all about the pregnancy, but Stratford hadn't known this.

At this point in the trial, Stratford claimed his innocence. Nine local clergy and tradesmen gave him 'a most excellent character for honesty, humanity and industry'. Mr Justice Parke summed up the case; reminded them that Isaac Kemp had searched Stratford's workshop, opposite the church of St Peter's Permountergate on King Street, on 3 March and found arsenic there in two papers; and then pointed out to the jury that the evidence incriminated Stratford.

The jury retired for five hours, then asked the judge to clear up one point for them: his answer was that no, there was no evidence that any flour was taken from the bag before Burgess made the dumpling.

The jury pronounced Stratford guilty of the crime of wilful murder; 'either to carry on that criminal connection which appears to have existed, or to conceal its result', he intended to murder Thomas Briggs. And although Stratford's plan didn't work, John Burgess died as a result: so Stratford was condemned to death, 'hanged by [his] neck until [he was] dead, and that [his] body be dissected.'

At midnight, Stratford was taken back to the gaol in an 'exhausted state' and given 'some trifling articles of nourishment' along with the bread and water that prisoners under sentence of death were supposed to have. Early the next morning, he was visited by Charles Millard, the prison chaplain. On the Saturday, one of the city sheriffs visited him, read him a section of the Bible from Isiah and persuaded him to confess the truth – Stratford was in tears at this point and blamed what happened on his addiction to 'reading infidel publications' (including Paine's *Age of Reason*), which he said caused 'the subversion of his principles and his final ruin'. Stratford did give the reporters of the *Norfolk Chronicle* a lengthy 'explanation of the circumstances which had led to his criminal connection with the woman Briggs' – but the report said they 'purposely omit to detail' the circumstances.

Stratford's confession was witnessed by C.F. Millard, the chaplain at the Norwich Gaol. Stratford said he'd only bought an ounce of arsenic from Cross (and paid him two pence). From talking to Jane Briggs, he knew she sent flour to Thomas in the workhouse. And she'd said to Stratford, 'What a blessing it would be if God would release him from his sufferings.' Stratford also knew that Jane was pregnant by him. He had a third of an ounce of crude arsenic, which he said he'd received from the person for whom he worked. He powdered it, sifted it through a piece of rag into some flour, put the flour into a bag, tied it up and took it to the workhouse at 11 a.m. on Wednesday 11 February. He gave it to Susanna Hook at the kitchen door and told her it was for Thomas Briggs.

Strangely, he claimed, 'It did not occur to me at this time that I was committing any crime, but when I went to bed, such terrors seized my mind that I could not sleep.' The next morning, he thought about going to the workhouse and taking the bag back – but then he thought it had probably been used by then so there was no point. Sadly, the flour hadn't been used at that point so if he'd gone with his conscience John Burgess wouldn't have died. Richard Lane of St George's enlarged upon this in Stratford's printed confession:

> *After he had left the bag of flour he was, upon reflection, conscience smitten at the heinousness of his crime, and he would have given worlds to have got the parcel back, but his effort to do so was paralized* [sic] *and he dared not make a disclosure to his paramour.*

Stratford admitted, 'My object was to destroy Briggs, from the fear that the exposure of my intimacy with the woman Briggs would break the peace between my wife and me.' Throughout, he'd always spoken of his wife as 'a loving, faithful, frugal and industrious wife; a virtuous woman, and an exemplary mother' and he was clearly fond of her.

He was also at pains to make sure that other people's names were cleared, by stating that he didn't use the arsenic he'd bought from Cross, and that 'Neither the woman Briggs nor any other person knew of my mixing the arsenic and flour, nor of my taking it to the Workhouse.'

Stratford's family came to visit him that afternoon – his wife, six children, his two brothers and their wives, and four 'more distant' relations. They stayed with him for almost two hours; though Stratford was moved to tears when his youngest daughter, 'scarcely four years of age', hugged him and asked him to go home with her 'to tea'. The same witness noted that his wife had 'an almost broken heart' and had lost a great deal of weight during the previous six months because of her grief at what had happened – but she also managed to comfort Stratford at his lowest hour.

The morning after the conviction, Mr Paraman, the governor of Norwich Gaol, went to London to find 'an experienced executioner'. He returned on the Sunday night and Stratford asked him to read the Bible to him. Later that day, Stratford told one of the gaolers that there was a pamphlet in a drawer at his house – 'One of Carlisle's blasphemous publications' (i.e. Richard Carlisle, revolutionary and advocate of Free Speech – Shelley wrote a letter about him in 1820 which was considered so dangerous that it wasn't actually published until 1990!) – and made the gaoler promise to find it and burn it so his children wouldn't find it and be affected.

Stratford couldn't rest, that night. By 5 a.m. the next morning, there were nearly three hundred people by the outer gates to the prison, waiting to view the execution, and 'the crowd kept rapidly increasing'. At ten, the bell rang for the chapel service. Stratford gave his hat, cap and comb to the three prisoners who'd shared his cell before the trial. After the service, he was led round the chapel to say goodbye to his fellow prisoners and was led back to his cell, where he prayed for a quarter of an hour and was visited by the mayor. He also had to put paid to another rumour circulating the city, that he'd set fire to the steam packet belonging to Mr Watts (his former employer). He added that he 'had used [his] best efforts at the moment of the conflagration to assist in extinguishing the flames'.

Just before twelve, the executioner, gaoler and head turnkey came to Stratford's cell to pinion his arms. He walked to the foot of the drop, 'walking firmly and with a steady countenance the whole way'. One unnamed person was 'weeping bitterly' for him, and Stratford said, 'Don't weep for me. I hope I shall soon be in heaven.' Ironically, Stratford had helped to build the gallows at the new gaol.

When the hangman put the rope round his neck, Stratford fretted that the knot was on the wrong side – presumably fearing that his death would therefore be slow and agonising. The hangman reassured him, then put the cap over Stratford's head. The executioner drew the bolt at the signal of a handkerchief during the chaplain's reading of the Lord's Prayer.

He was the first man to be executed on the roof of the new city gaol just outside St Giles' Gates (now the location of St John's Roman Catholic Cathedral), so a huge crowd gathered to see the execution. The *Norfolk*

Trial and Execution,

LIFE, CHARACTER, and BEHAVIOUR of JOHN STRATFORD, who was Executed at the City Gaol, of Norwich, on Monday, August 17th, 1829, for the wilful Murder of John Burgess, by Poison.

The Trial which commenced on Friday Morning last about nine o'clock and lasted till five in the afternoon, excited the most extraordinary interest in the minds of the inhabitants of this City, as the wretched culprit was a man generally known, and (until the fatal connexion between him and the infamous woman, Briggs, the wife of another man) was respected as an industrious, careful man, and much esteemed by his employers as an ingenious workman, he being a Whitesmith by Trade. At one time he kept the sign of the Swan, in King-street, which after a year or two he left, and continued to follow his business as a Smith, by which he supported a wife and six children, that he was infinitely attached to, till the unfortunate connexion that he formed with this woman, when so infatuated did he become by his criminal attachment to this disgrace to her sex, that he sacrificed, without remorse, the peace and happiness of his family, to prefer the embraces of this wanton ; and not satisfied with the degree of guilt in which he was thus involved, he formed the diabolical plan of taking away the life of the poor afflicted creature, her husband, who was a pauper in the Workhouse, in this City, who for this last year has not taken any thing but thick milk through a tube on account of his having a cancer in the throat, for which purpose he procured some arsenic, and mixing it with some flour, left it with a servant girl in the Work-house, to be delivered to Briggs, the injured husband of the object of his attachment ; but it pleased the Almighty to disappoint his intention in this respect, as the flour remained untouched by Briggs for three weeks, but unfortunately he requested his Nurse [Rhoda Burgess] to take it for her own use, as he had no occasion for it, and thought it a pity the flour should be spoiled, she accordingly took it, and made it up into dumplings, of which she and her husband [the deceased John Burgess] did eat, as did also her son and two other persons, who were all soon affected with vomitings, and other symptoms indicative of their having taken poison. Medical assistance being called and every assistance offered which the case demanded, they all recovered, except the unfortunate husband John Burgess, who lingered in the greatest agony for a few hours and then expired, it being ascertained by the Surgeons, that his death was occasioned by arsenic being mixed with the flour of which he had eaten.

The Prisoner was immediately apprehended, and the girl swore to him being the person of whom she received the flour in the Work-house kitchen, and he was in consequence committed to the City Gaol till the Assizes, and when put on his Trial, pleaded " Not Guilty."

A number of witnesses were then called, whose testimony tended so clearly to convict the Prisoner, [more especially the woman who was the original cause of his guilt] that no doubt remained of his culpability, and although he had assistance of two Counsellors from London, with the well-known professional abilities of Mr. Palmer, & t.Stephens, Norwich, the circumstances were so clear against him, and the crime so clearly established, that Lord Chief Justice Park in summing up the evidence, pointed out to the Jury, how every part of the evidence corroborated to criminate the Prisoner beyond the possibility of a doubt. Notwithstanding which, the Jury after retiring, remained five hour in consultation, before they returned a verdict of Guilty.

The Learned Judge immediately passed the awful sentence of the law, and the people from the windows of the Court-room proclaimed the event of the Trial to the anxious multitude outside, who had waited the result with the most intense interest till 11 o'clock at night.— We understand, that since his condemnation, he has confessed his Guilt, and no one knew what he did

He was therefore, pursuant to his sentence, brought out for Execution, on Monday, amidst a vast concourse of spectators, being the first that has suffered at this place of Execution.

BEWARE OF INFIDELITY.

With what earnestness might he say,

How truly awful must be the situation of that man who denies the truth of God's Holy Word.—He who can be so daringly wicked must shut himself out of all happiness in both worlds.— All is dark in this, and in the next, blackness and darkness for ever. It is this unbelief which has proved the ruin of thousands, and for this number's are fearfully anticipating the day of Judgment, when all unbelievers shall be cast into the land of anguish, from whence the God of their idolatry can never deliver them. It is unbelief which leads mankind to the perpetration of those crimes which render them a pest to society, and brings them to an untimely end.

If men would believe the Bible, they would not continue to practice those sins which are too prevalent in this our highly favoured country. The Sabbath breaker would obey the command and keep holy the Sabbath day. The Thief would remember God has said, Thou shalt not steal. The whore-monger, the idolater, and the liar, would stop in their mad career, knowing such must have their portion in the lake of fire and brimstone, and the Murderer would immediately drop his arm which was raised to take away his brother's life, knowing that God has said, Thou shalt do no Murder.

My soul lies humbled in the dust,
And owns thy dreadful sentence just ;
Look down, O Lord, with pitying eye;
And save the soul condemn'd to die;

Shew pity, Lord, O Lord forgive,
Let a repenting rebel live :
Are not thy mercies large and free ?
May not a sinner trust in thee ?

My crimes are great, but don't surpass
The power and glory of thy grace :
Great God, thy nature hath no bound;
So let thy pardoning love be found.

O wash my soul from every sin,
And make my guilty conscience clean,
Here on my heart the burthen lies,
And past offences pain my eyes.

My sips with shame my sins confess
Against thy law, against thy grace :
Lord, should thy judgment grow severe,
I am condemn'd, but thou art clear.

Yet here a trembling sinner, Lord,
Whose hope still hovering round thy word,
Would light on some sweet promise there,
Some sure support against despair.

R. LANE, PRINTER ST. GEORGE'S, NORWICH.

Gallows broadside for John Stratford. © Norfolk County Council Library and Information Service

Chronicle reported that the crowd 'extended back into St Giles' Street as far as it was possible to catch a glimpse of the gallows'. According to *The Times*, the tower of St Giles' Church was let for £2 and spectators gathered on the battlements of the church steeple, while the owner of a field overlooking the site posted a note in the gateway: 'Admission in here: 2d each', and made enough money from the occasion to pay a year's rent.

Death mask of John Stratford at Norwich Castle.

After the execution, Stratford's body was then taken down, stripped and taken to the Guildhall in a cart for exposure to public view – several thousand people (women as well as men!) went to see it over the course of two hours. His body was then taken to the Norfolk and Norwich hospital for dissection; Mr Mazzotti, the modeller, took a cast from the head and neck 'for craniological purposes' – and a phrenologist mentioned that 'Stratford's brain is one of the finest and firmest that I ever saw dissected'. The surgeon Mr Cross delivered several anatomical lectures on Stratford's body, to what appears to be large audiences, including 'a great many medical pupils'.

Lane commented in the *Confession*:

He is a man who has read much, and possessed an intelligent mind... he is a smith by trade, and supposed to be the most ingenious machanic [sic] in Norwich... He said his downfall was primarily to reading THE AGE OF REASON and the recent work of Charlile [sic], and the secondary cause is my illicit connection with that abandoned woman Briggs... His 90-year-old father lives to lament him.

Shortly after Stratford's death, J.J. Gurney published a tract about him. He echoed Lane's comments, saying that Stratford was 'endued with excellent sense and good natural talents, and his mind was more cultivated than is generally the case with persons of the labouring class'. Stratford was known as 'one of the ablest working mechanics in the city', diligent, and 'for many long years a good husband, and a kind considerate parent'. According to Gurney,

> *Stratford, under the fatal guidance of false principles – under the pernicious tuition of a Payne and a Carlisle – renounces public worship; breaks the Sabbath; connects himself with gamblers; becomes the companion of sinners, faithless to an exemplary wife, an adulterer, and in the end, a Murderer.*

But it doesn't answer the question: why did Stratford really want to kill Thomas Briggs? Was it because he'd fallen in love with Jane (bearing in mind his own avowal that he didn't want to 'break peace' with his wife) or was it a mercy killing because Thomas Briggs was his friend and was clearly suffering? Was Jane the real murderess (and she'd certainly have a motive – her husband was seriously ill, a pauper in the workhouse, and until he died she wouldn't be able to remarry and put her financial situation back on a sound footing) and did Stratford perjure himself to save her?

We will never know. But the end result was tragedy, a fourteen-hour trial, and a public hanging.

The Plum-cake Poisoner:

MARY WRIGHT, 1833

Mary Wright's case is particularly sad – to the modern eye, it's obvious that she suffered from postnatal depression and possibly even its most severe form, puerpal psychosis, as well as some form of mental illness. However, at the time medical knowledge wasn't quite advanced enough to help her. At her trial, Mary's lawyer tried to plead that her actions were driven by insanity, but failed to establish the case. And the sheer desperation of the events that happened immediately after the sentence was pronounced were described in *The Times* as 'excit[ing] great interest in court; no one, probably, of the spectators having ever before witnessed a similar scene.'

Mary Wright was placed at the bar, charged with the wilful murder of her husband William by mixing up arsenic with his food. She pleaded not guilty.

The first few witnesses set the scene for her marriage: Mary was twenty-eight and her husband William was aged somewhere between thirty and forty. William was employed by Mr Mack as a teamsterman (i.e. a full-time employee who looked after the horses and carts) and lived with his wife and his father-in-law.

Two colleagues – William Snell and William Hales – testified that Wright loaded a waggon with corn around 7 a.m. on Saturday 1 December 1832, intending to go to Cley. That was the last time Snell saw him; but Hales saw him in Cley at 2 p.m., just before he was due to come home again. At that point William Wright was 'lying upon a granary on some sacks', complaining of pains throughout his body. Hales helped Wright into a pub, and somewhere before 3 p.m. sent for Mr Buck, the local surgeon, who lived at Cley.

Charles Buck confirmed that he'd been sent for on the Saturday 'to attend a person taken sick at the pub,' and saw him at around 3 p.m. At the time William Wright was in violent pain, with 'his extremities quite cold', and had been vomiting; the surgeon suspected cholera, which was rife in the district at the time. He came back an hour later and Bell the landlady and Claxton the nurse said that the patient had been vomiting;

Buck advised them to save the vomit and show it to him, next time. He came back twice more that day and saw the vomit, and was still convinced the cause of illness was cholera.

On Sunday at noon, Mary Wright went to the surgeon and asked him to come and see her husband, because she thought he was dying. Buck went with her to the pub and saw William there – confirming that he'd seen the man the day before. He saw William twice more that day and described his condition as 'weak', with a pulse that was 'quick and weak'; William was 'full of pain' but the doctor couldn't see anything peculiar about his skin or body. The last time he came to see William on the Sunday, he couldn't feel a heartbeat and pronounced the patient dead.

As with most cases of suspected cholera, the body was buried as soon as possible – in William's case, on the Monday. But Mary's father died on the same day as the funeral, 'under very suspicious circumstances' said *The Times*, and because he'd lived with Mary and her husband suspicion fell on her. William was exhumed, and Buck was called to examine William on the Thursday 'in the chancel of Wighton church'. He examined the body and said it was 'not tense, tympanic or swelled', but he removed the stomach and noticed a 'peculiar inflammation confined to the curvature of the stomach.' He took the remains personally to Mr

Wighton church where William Wright's body was examined.

Cross, and his pupil opened it; the contents were 'grumous brown semi-fluid', and Buck thought 'he must have taken some acrid matter of a ponderous nature'. Although the symptoms he'd noticed in Wright on the Saturday were similar to those of cholera – cold extremities, a weak and quick pulse, with bodily pain' the dissected stomach looked as if Wright had ingested arsenic. Buck put three or four ounces of the stomach contents in a bottle and delivered it to Mr Bell, a chemist at Wells, for analysis.

Cross agreed that cholera was prevalent in the area in the time, but the stomach he examined didn't look as if it belonged to someone who'd died from cholera. The stomach lining was inflamed 'at the cardiac end and the curvature of the stomach'. Cross examined the stomach contents by sight but not chemically, and saw a dense, dark green fluid with a few dried currants floating in it.

It began to look as if Wright had been poisoned through eating a plum cake.

Mr Bell took the stand and testified that he'd been a chemist for a quarter of a century. He examined the fluid and did several tests – and every chemical he used pointed to the presence of arsenic. When he tested the fluid with sulphurated hydrogen there was a golden precipitate; with ammoniated sulphate of copper, there was a light grass green precipitate; with ammoniated nitrate of silver, it was light gold, and with carbonate of copper, it was light yellow green. He also noted the currants in the stomach contents. He admitted that he hadn't known many cases of arsenic poisoning and the chemical tests weren't infallible – but added, 'I have always found them correct.' He also stated that no animal or vegetable matter could product the same results with the chemical tests.

The coroner's jury had already returned verdicts of wilful murder on the bodies. But the prosecution had to prove the link with Mary. Several witnesses had said they'd never heard of any quarrels between husband and wife, so what was her motive?

Ann Cross, another employee of Mr Mack, shed some light on it for the court. A month before Wright died, Mary asked Ann for poison to get rid of some mice. The week before Wright's death, they went to Walsingham together, and Mary was distraught – she thought her husband had become much too friendly with Mrs Bright, one of their neighbours. He'd given Mary half a fish, but he'd given the other half to Mrs Bright. Mary told Ann, 'I would stick a knife in him before he should let a neighbour have a part of it, as he had more regard for her [the neighbour] than for his wife.' On Thursday 29 November, Mary told Eliza Cook, 'I should not mind running a knife through him or doing his business in some other way.'

On Friday 30 November, Mary borrowed 6d from a neighbour, Mary Hastings; she said she needed the money to buy some stuff to make a pocket for her husband's coat, as he was off to Cley with the team in the morning. A little later that day, Sarah Hastings went to Wells with Mary to the druggist Sarah Leslie's shop. Mary asked for 7d-worth of opium and 6d-worth of arsenic; Mrs Leslie sold her the opium but refused to sell her the arsenic. Next, they went to William Read Pridgeon's chemist shop, but there were several people in there so Mary refused to go in. She told Sarah that if she had gone in, she would have asked for 6d-worth of arsenic for Frost the ratcatcher – though, in court, Abraham Frost testified that he'd never asked Mary to get any arsenic for him.

Next, they went to the chemist shop of Richard Bell, and asked him for 6d-worth of arsenic. Bell asked her why she wanted it. 'To poison rats,' she said. He told her that 6d-worth was 'enough to poison all the rats in the country', and then she said she'd take 3d-worth. Bell duly weighed out 3 ounces of arsenic for her.

On the way back to Wighton, Mary asked Sarah Hastings how much arsenic it would take to kill someone. Then she asked her not to say they'd been to Wells. She said to Mary Hastings that she'd bought some suet from Mr Leader's to make a short cake.

'What, then, you've a short cake for dinner?' asked Mary.

'No, not for dinner. I shall have to look for my husband and father, and shall make a short cake sure enough, but not for dinner.'

Later that afternoon she bought half a pound of currants from Ursula Bailey's grocery shop in the village – the same type of currants found in the stomachs of her husband and father.

There was a definite chain of circumstances – one that linked Mary to the murders.

The defence team put forward a plea of insanity, and the cross-examination brought out pertinent facts. Neighbour Mary Hastings testified that Mary Wright's mother had been in the Bethel (the lunatic asylum in Norwich), and nurse Mary Frost confirmed that Mary Wright's mother had been insane and put in the asylum for eighteen months before her death, and 'was quite crazy before she went to Bedlam'. She added that she'd spent two months with Mary Wright 'after her last confinement', the previous Easter. According to Mary Frost, Mary Wright was 'very strange in her manner', and had set fire to the tablecloth and chairs, as well as to her child's cradle and the bedding. She also refused to nurse the baby, although previously she'd been very attached to her family; she cried over the child and used to 'walk about wildly for hours together', so Mary Frost was afraid to leave the mother and child together. 'She's never been in her right mind since the confinement,' said Mary Frost.

Then she gave even more telling evidence: at harvest, Mary Wright went to the nurse and said she was going to gather some kidney beans and 'invite all the better folk to have a frolic'. Then she went home and got a razor and put it in her pocket – but her husband followed her to the fields, so she turned back. She frequently told Mary Frost that she 'had seen the devil sitting a-top of a tree'; and although she'd always been very neat she hadn't been able to bear having the house cleaned since the baby's birth.

It's not clear whether William really had been taking comfort outside his marriage or whether Mary had imagined it; however, Mary's mental state would definitely have put a strain on the marriage, and the legal and moral strictures of the time meant that they were both stuck in a marriage that wasn't quite working, with no way out. Nowadays, Mary would have access to psychiatric help and William too would be given support; back in the 1830s they had no help or hope. The marriage couldn't be dissolved, either; a court case would have cost more money than they had, and William had no grounds on which to divorce Mary.

Mr Cross, an eminent Norwich surgeon, testified that madness could be hereditary. He added that 'childbearing is apt to produce insanity, mostly temporary,' and that 'the prisoner shewed indications of being of unsound mind'. He qualified that, however, by saying that this was only during the period Mary Frost had spoken of, and as Frost had quitted her post at Michaelmas, two months before William Wright died, it didn't apply to the time when Mary Wright allegedly poisoned her husband. Other witnesses said that they hadn't seen Mary Wright show any signs of insanity at all. However, given the stigma of having a relative 'in the Bethel', it's likely that Mary's father and husband both tried to cover up as much as they could.

Mary's fate was sealed.

The judge summed up and said that the jury's task was to say if Mary Wright administered poison to her husband, either in a currant cake or otherwise; if they thought she did, they needed to say whether she was 'in a sound state of mind' at the time the crime was committed, 'so as to be able to distinguish between right and wrong'.

The jury took only a few minutes' consultation to pronounce her guilty and of sound mind, and the judge pronounced the death sentence; according to the reports in the *Norfolk Chronicle*, Mary immediately 'fell into an hysteric fit'.

Then her defence lawyer, Mr Taylor, caused a sensation by speaking up and asking for a stay of execution because Mary Wright was pregnant. According to the law at the time, an 'innocent unborn child shall not be deprived of existence on account of the crime of the parent'.

The judge asked the Sheriff to find him a jury of matrons; twelve married women were duly sworn in at the box and the judge directed them to 'try according to the best of their ability and skill whether the prisoner was pregnant with a "quick" child or not'. They retired and examined Mary for an hour; their verdict was that she wasn't pregnant, but Mary was finally respited with a certificate signed by three accouchers – Messrs Cross, Scott and Johnson. She gave birth to a girl on 11 July, and her sentence was commuted from the death penalty to transportation for life.

However, she died in Norwich Castle on 1 November, before she could be transported.

Wilful Murder of a Child:
JAMES SOUTH, 1834

The case of James South is another where we'll never know the truth; there just wasn't enough evidence to prove anything. Back in 1834, the local police force was in its very early stages and certainly didn't have modern forensic tests available to them. Whether what happened in this case was murder or misadventure, nobody will ever know.

On 1 August 1834, 39-year-old James South was indicted for the wilful murder of his illegitimate child by poison on 16 March 1834.

South was a labourer living in Poringland, and for the past three years he'd worked for Alderman Thurtell as his second teamsman (or horse-keeper). In 1832, the *Norfolk Chronicle and Norwich Gazette* reported, he'd 'formed illicit intercourse' with a widow called Mary Serjeant, who also lived in Poringland. In Christmas 1833, she gave birth to a daughter; she 'duly affiliated the child upon' South and the case was brought before two justices, who agreed that he was the father and ordered him to pay 1 shilling and 6 pence for its support every week. (This is only about £5.57 per week in modern money – but bear in mind that the average wage for a labourer in Norfolk in 1834 was only 8 shillings and 6 pence a week, so it was actually 17 per cent of his income.) Mrs Serjeant had three sons living with her, the eldest being about 13 or 14 years old.

South complained to Mrs Serjeant about the expense of the child support; in court, she claimed that he'd said to her, about ten days before the murder, that

Farmland at Poringland

'she had the best end of the staff a good deal, and he was a deal worse off about it than she was'. So it seemed that James South had a motive for the murder: the baby was a drain on his income.

But did he really resent his daughter that much?

Elizabeth, the wife of George Worman who kept the local pub, said that when the baby was born, her son was 'passing his jokes' with South and called him 'old father'. South's response was: 'Oh, don't trouble me, it would be a good thing if it were dead.' However, Mrs Worman said she understood this as a 'joke – and the more so as he seemed so fond of the poor thing.' To modern ears, the 'joke' is remarkably unfunny; however, what people find humorous changes over time, and Mrs Worman added that many married men said the same thing – so it seems unlikely that South actually meant it.

Mary Serjeant testified that South lived in the same house as Mr Beckett, who was Alderman Thurtell's steward. She explained that 'being engaged with his labours during the week' he didn't visit her or the child on weekdays, but tended to visit them on Sundays and spent time with them then. She'd known him for ten years; the child was 'cross, sometimes stilled by being taken into his arms.' So clearly South did have feelings for his daughter: he visited her every week (as much as he could, working long hours and not living with Mrs Serjeant) and was able to stop her crying with a cuddle. Hardly the actions of a man who wanted to kill a baby.

South's fellow horsekeeper (or first teamsman), Henry Stone, said that on the day the baby was born Mrs Serjeant 'was laid bad' and South told him if Mrs Serjeant died, he would take the baby to his mother, 'give it all the learning he could afford' and 'make it quite a comfort to him in his old age'. Stone testified that South was 'always very fond of the child' – so was it really likely that he would murder his baby?

Mrs Serjeant's testimony at the trial went through the events of the day. On 16 March 1834, South called to ask how the baby was, but didn't stay long. At about half-past four that afternoon he called again. Mrs Serjeant had the baby in her lap and had just finished suckling it; South kissed the baby and told Mrs Serjeant to go to Mr Worman's for three pints of beer as he didn't feel well and would like some egg cordial. Mrs Serjeant said in court that 'I saw no egg' for making the cordial; he'd never sent her anywhere for beer before, either. She demurred and said that Mr Worman's was too far, so she would go to Mr Thetford's at the White Hart as it was nearer. She put the baby in the cradle, and it was absolutely fine.

Twenty minutes later, she returned with the beer to find the baby out of the cradle in South's arms, very sick 'and frothing violently at the mouth'. We would expect one of them to want to call the doctor, but South's actions were somewhat odd here: he asked Mrs Sergeant to get their neighbour Mrs Brighty and ask her to come over for some beer. Even if he couldn't afford to call the doctor out, why on earth have a drink with the neighbours?

Mrs Serjeant and Mrs Brighty were back in the room with South and the baby within a couple of minutes. South said, 'Come, Mrs Brighty, and have some beer, and ask Mrs Serjeant to drink; I never did ax her to drink before, but I will ax her now.'

They drank the beer – cold, so Mrs Serjeant clearly didn't make it into an egg cordial – and meanwhile the baby was getting worse, its 'sickness and foaming having much increased'. South cried out, 'Lord have mercy on me! What's come to the child? If it dies, folks will say I gave it something!'

Mrs Serjeant replied, 'Mercy on us! Who would say so?'

South didn't reply but went to his father's house a few doors away. Meanwhile, the little girl grew weaker and sicker, and eventually Mrs Serjeant sent for him. He came back and said to Mrs Brighty that they should send for the doctor; she responded, 'It's too late, as the child could live no time.' The baby died at 7.45 p.m., about three and three-quarter hours after the sickness first came on.

According to Mrs Serjeant, the baby 'threw up a small quantity of bread and milk'. She said that there was a basin of bread and milk in the pantry; she had give the baby some of it at midday but not later, and there weren't any spoons near it. When she came back with the beer, she noticed that the pantry door was open, although she'd left it shut earlier. She asked South why the door was open, and he claimed he'd been there to get a bit of bread and meat.

'Nay, that can't be, for the bread is in this room in the mealtub,' she said.

His response was that he had his own bread in his pocket but no meat. Mrs Serjeant testified that yes, there was a pig's face in the pantry, but she didn't give any of it to South.

So had the child's bread and milk been poisoned? It seems not, because Mrs Serjeant drank the milk from the basin, the next day and suffered no ill effects; she put her bread into Mrs Brighty's swilltub and the pigs were fine.

Under examination, Mrs Serjeant admitted that the baby 'was a very crying and cross child'. Although she'd left the child wide awake in the cradle when she went to fetch the beer, South was probably holding it when she returned because it had been crying. She mentioned that 'one mode of stilling a child's cries [was] to take it in the arms and walk about the room with it, as the prisoner was doing', and admitted that once before she'd left the child alone with South. He was 'uniformly kind to and fond of it, and nursed it and kissed it whenever he visited her with great affection'. Again, this is at odds with the behaviour of someone who intended to kill a child.

Mrs Brighty, the neighbour, corroborated Mrs Serjeant's account. She added that when the baby was 'at its worst' South cuddled it and 'wept quite sad over it' and said 'he should not like to lose it, though folks did say he wished it, and that was as true as God'.

As was usual in the case of a death where poison was suspected, the surgeons were called in to do a post-mortem and examine the contents of the stomach. Richard Merry of Shottisham [sic], Richard Griffin of Norwich and William Stark of Norwich testified that they had examined the contents of the baby's stomach and perfomed tests. The tests involved sulphurated hydrogen gas, sulphuret of potash and sulphate of ammoni-acal copper; all showed the presence of arsenic. Finally, 'the grand and indisputable experiment was performed' and arsenic was produced.

So the child was clearly killed with poison. But who did it, and how?

Five weeks before the child's death, South asked Ward the ratcatcher for some poison to get rid of rats in his dad's pigsty, because the rats ate more than the pig did. Ward gave him quarter of an ounce of arsenic and told him how to set the bait with it – all he had to do was mix the poison with a little barley meal to bait it for the rats. He should keep it out of the pig's reach as it was a 'rank poison' and would kill the pig immediately. Though Ward testified that he didn't actually tell South that the poison was arsenic, just that it was poison. A witness for prosecution confirmed that South's father had a pigsty and complained that it was overrun with rats: so South had a valid reason for asking for the poison.

He wasn't the only one. Three weeks before the baby died, Mr Beckett the steward had asked Thomas Lee the ratcatcher for a quantity of crude arsenic and 'prepared arsenic paste' to destroy the rats on his property. Lee – who'd known South for three or four years – said that he made the paste out of flour and milk. 'I don't make it up strong for the rats will not take it if I do.'

Beckett made the paste into small pea-sized balls, laid them on a saucer and placed the saucer in a hole in the fence next to the muckheap in a field known as 'the eleven acres'. Mrs Serjeant's eldest son (who didn't testify at the trial) was 'keeping crows' in that field; Beckett's theory was that the boy might have found the balls and taken them home to his mother and put them in the pantry, or even accidentally dropped them in the milk.

Meanwhile, Beckett put the residue of the poison into the box of a drill in the coach-house. South and Henry Stone had access to the room as they kept the corn for their horses there. South's corn bin stood next to the drill box and his key would unlock both the corn bin and the drill box. According to Beckett, South knew that there was poison in the coach house but not what it was.

South may or may not have had a motive (depending on whose comments you believe), he had access to poison both at work and at his father's pigsty, and he was left alone with the child.

But there wasn't any evidence showing that he administered the poison, or how he did it.

The girl who'd testified to the rats in the pigsty said that she'd taken the baby to South's mother on the day it died, but didn't let it out of her sight. She added that when the baby was ill in the evening, she took it glass of red wine but it couldn't swallow.

South said that he'd never seen any arsenic to his life, as far as he knew: which could well be the truth, as both Beckett and Ward said they hadn't told South that the poison was arsenic.

Plenty of people testified to South's good character. The head teamsman, Henry Stone, said he'd known South for 10 years and he had a good honest character. Beckett the steward agreed, adding that South was fond of children. Mrs Worman, the publican's wife, said she'd known South for 20 years and his character was kind and upright. Several local worthies also gave South a character reference.

The jury conferred for nearly two hours, then retired for three hours. Their verdict was that the child died of poison, but they couldn't say who had administered it. South was not guilty.

The Times was a little more scathing about the episode: 'On this Assize circuit not a single sentence of death had been passed, let alone an execution, despite trials for some appalling crimes.'

The Burnham Poisoners:

FRANCES BILLING, CATHERINE FRAREY
AND PETER TAYLOR, 1835–6

The trial of the Burnham Poisoners in August 1835 shocked the county – and shocked the whole country, too, as *The Times* ran a series of reports on the scandals. The sensational story had all the elements of high drama: adultery, alleged witchcraft and murder. To add insult to injury, it happened in the area where Nelson, the county's hero, was born – and his victory at Trafalgar was still strong in living memory.

There were several counts for the trial. Firstly, the murder of Mary, the wife of Peter Taylor, by administering arsenic; Frarey was named as the principal and Billing as accessory before the fact. Secondly, both Billing and Frarey were arraigned for the murder of Robert Frarey, Catherine's husband, by administering poison to him in porter. Taylor managed to avoid the 1835 trial, to the disgust of the spectators, but was finally indicted as accessory before the fact to murder of his wife Mary in April 1836.

Local opinion was sharply divided and the polarisation showed in the local papers. The *Norwich Mercury* took the side of Taylor, saying that he was previously of good character but was led astray by Billing, whereas the *Norfolk Chronicle and Norwich Gazette* lambasted Taylor as 'profligate' and said that he'd been the one to lead Billing astray and turned her away from the church. A pamphlet written shortly after the executions – *The Burnham Murders, printed and sold by J Riches, News-Agent and Bookseller, St George's Bridge Street, Norwich: an account of the lives, trials and execution of Peter Taylor, Frances Billing and Catherine Frarey* – took the side of Taylor, calling Billing 'a female of loose character' and adding that Frarey was the same. It goes so far as to say that Frarey 'appears long to have been a woman of loose character, though of no personal attractiveness whatever, and her chief study seems to have been how she might most successfully carry on her intrigues with the men, married or single.'

But the story was more complicated than an adulterous affair or two – it seemed that the Burnham poisoners had other targets in mind, too. *The*

The Trial and Execution,

Of Francis BILLINGS, aged 46, & Catherine FRAREY, aged 40,

Who were Executed on the Castle-Hill, at Norwich, on Monday, Aug. 10, 1835, Billings for the Murder of Mary Taylor, wife of Peter Taylor, of Burnham, by administering Poison, and Frarey for the Murder of her own Husband, by Poison, also in the same place.

THE Trial of these two miserable Women who have been so long in Prison, excited such a degree of interest, that the Court on Friday morning was crowded to excess. The cruel and diabolical nature of their Guilt inspired such universal horror and detestation, that Country People from the parts where these Culprits dwelt flocked in numbers to witness their trial. The Children and other Relations of the Prisoners stood trembling in the court in awful expectation of the event, that would tear these miserable Mothers from their sight for ever. The unhappy woman Billings have been the mother of 14 Children, 9 of them now alive, most of whom were in the court in a fainting state during the greater part of the trial of their miserable Parent. The trial of these wretched women lasted many hours, during which 17 witnesses were examined whose testimony brought the Guilt of the Prisoners so forcibly home to them, that the Jury after a most impressive charge from the Learned Judge found them both Guilty of their separate crimes. The verdict was received in the profoundest silence, and the moment the Foreman of the Jury pronounced the word Guilty, the Paleness of Death overspread the countenances of both Prisoners, and they were with difficulty kept from falling. And when the Judge proceeded to pass the dreadful sentence of Death, Shrieks of Horror were heard in different parts of the court proceeding from the Friends and Relations of the miserable condemn'd Women, who were both taken out of court in a senseless state, and convey'd back to their Cells. On Saturday the children and other relations of the Prisoners were permitted to visit them, to take their last farewell, and the scene that took place on this melancholy occasion, it is not in our power to describe; two fine young women the daughters of the prisoner Billings hung round the neck of their miserable Parent in speechless agony. Whilst the wretched Mother, who although in other respects so Guilty, was always infinitely fond of her children exclaimed " Oh my dear, dear, children, tis for you I shall feel, as for myself I have merited my Fate, but to be torn from you by an ignominious Death, to part from all my dear children, to end my Life on a Scaffold, tear my very heartstrings asunder, Oh wretched Mother, & is this to be the last time, I shall fold you to my miserable bosom, what cruel Fate could tempt me to commit the horrid Deed that have brought me to this dreadful End! again she clasp'd them in her arms, whilst the voices of all three were choaked by their Sobs in silent anguish, the daughters clung to their miserable Parent, and groan'd in anguish, those who were permitted to witness this Scene, could bear it no longer without giving vent to their feelings by a Shower of Tears! The woman Frarey who have always been nearly in a state of distraction ever since her first being taken to Walsingham, now appear to feel in a tenfold degree, all the horror of her situation. She could scarcely recollect her nearest Friends, but continually kept exclaiming in a frantic manner, Oh my Murdered Husband! Soon shall I appear at that Bar where thou wilt confront me with the diabolical act of thy cruel murder. Oh! then wilt thou reproach me with thine untimely death. My Judges were merciful and gave me time to prepare for Death, but I wretched woman shew no mercy to thee, but sent thee to an untimely Grave, without allowing thee one hour to make thy peace with God; but soon shall my writhing and suffering frame be expos'd to the Gaze of the multitude who will witness without regret the miserable Death of so wretched a Murderer as myself: And Oh, may my awful End be a warning to all who see and read of me.

After these afflicting scenes their Friends and Relations took their last and Final Leave of the unhappy Women, and were with difficulty separated for ever from their heartbroken and Forlorn Culprits, who passed the rest of their time till the period of their Execution, in unfeigned repentance, every opportunity was afforded to them for the Spiritual assistance so necessary in their unhappy condition, and their last hours were devoted to offering up the most fervent prayer for their Guilty Souls! On Monday morning at an early hour the Spectators began to assemble, and by the time the unfortunate women ascended the Drop, it was computed that not less than 10,000 People were assembled. At the sight of the unhappy Culprits, who were both comely women, an universal feeling of commiseration pervaded the breasts of the Spectators. At the sight of the awful preparations for their dreadful Doom, they were with great difficulty kept from fainting, and were obliged to be supported to the Fatal Drop, which after a few moments spent in prayer fell, and the wretched Culprits were Launched into Eternity !!!

All you that these poor Wretches rend behold,
One hour ago in health! one Dead and Cold!
Their vicious passions brought them to their end,
And to the warning of their fate attend.

Two Guilty Murderers, many years it have been
Since a woman Executed here have been;
An awful dreadful sight that none behold,
But at the Spectacle, their blood run Cold.

What anguish must that wretched Billings feel,
Her 'though lose in Life she lov'd her Children well:
Nine of them in their prime to mourn her Fate,
Who loved their mother 'though her crime was great.

Two of them smiling Babes of tender years,
Who not as yet have thought of worldly cares;
Whose artless innocence, but little know
The Crime that work'd their mother's overthrow.

Who can their tender wants so well supply,
Or where's the stranger like a Mother's Eye;
That wretched mother who Alas is gone,
And to her offspring never can return.

The other wretch that suffered by her side,
The woman Frarey deep in Guilt was dy'd;
Or else she had never mix'd the fatal Dose,
That in the Grave her Husband's life did close

Ah what could tempt her guilty murderous hand,
Thus unprepar'd her Husband's Soul, to send
Before his Maker! that she might live in his,
Which at last brought her to this untimely end.

Ah who can view their Bodies after death,
That lately saw them full of Life and Breath;
Now for Dissection laid, and Public Shew,
Oh awful warning dreadful sight of woe !

May such a Spectacle a Lesson be,
To shun the Path of Vice and Misery;
And though with crimes their Guilty souls are stain'd,
May both by Christ's redeeming arms accept't be saved.

[Walker, Printer, Orford-Hill, Norwich.]

Gallows broadside for Frances Billings and Catherine Frarey.

Times said that the village of Burnham Market and its vicinity 'have for the last week been in the most dreadful state of excitement' because of three murders and 'a plan for taking away the lives of several other people'. The *Norwich Mercury* added that 'these infatuated and abandoned women were in the habit of consulting reputed witches in the expectation that these hags would by their incantations remove those whom they afterwards took more effectual means to destroy'. There was even a ring of alleged witches; though *The Times* was quick to point out a large dose of quackery surrounding the witchcraft myth: 'Two of these mischievous pretenders to supernatural agency reside at Wells, one at Burnham and one at Sall[e].'

Catherine Frarey lodged at the house of Mrs Lake with her husband and three children, next door to the Taylors. She had a reputation of having a string of lovers, and rumour had it that she was very friendly with Hannah Shorten, the 'witch of Wells', who told fortunes and made love potions. One of these potions involved mixing arsenic with salt and throwing it on a fire – and Shorten had been implicated in telling the fortune of Mary Wright, who'd poisoned her husband a couple of years before in nearby Wighton.

Peter Taylor was a journeyman shoemaker by trade, although he had a reputation of being lazy (unlike his wife, who worked in the same industry as a shoebinder) and worked occasionally as a barber and waiter. The *Burnham Murderers* pamphlet mentions that Mary Taylor 'has since Whitsuntide entirely maintained her husband by her industry, he having no work' – however, they both worked for the same employer, shoemaker Mr Anderson of Burnham. The pamphlet grudgingly admitted that 'he was said not to be very fond of work', but then claimed he was 'considered sober and steady' until 1833, when he met Frances Billing, the neighbour on the other side of his cottage, and started having an affair with her.

According to *The Times*, the Taylors were both around 47 years old and had no children but 'lived very comfortably together'; Billing meanwhile was 50, and had fourteen children (of whom nine were still alive). The *Burnham Murderers* pamphlet adds that her eldest child was 26 and the youngest 12.

Their respective spouses weren't happy about the adulterous relationship. Mary Taylor asked her husband to end it, though he ignored her; Billing's husband James meanwhile resorted to sorting things out with his fists. He caught them 'in the back room with the door locked' in July

1833 and hit his wife. Her reaction was to see the magistrate and get a warrant out against him the next day; but then they made it up. Trouble flared again in November 1833 when James found them in the privy together; this time, he 'took Taylor by the collar, tore his shirt and gave him a good thrashing.' His wife's response was to swear against him and he was bound over to keep the peace.

At the trial, Henry Nash, the local chemist and druggist, confirmed this when he said he'd attended the recent petty sessions when James Billing was charged with ill usage to Frances. James's excuse for beating his wife was that he'd caught her with Peter Taylor in the privy (there was a shared external facility for the three cottages); Frances agreed that they'd been there together but said that they were 'there for no improper purpose'. Billing's son Joseph testified at the trial that his father was jealous whenever he saw Frances and Peter talking, so Joseph asked his mother to 'break off all acquaintance' with Peter – but she refused. In the meantime, according to *The Times*, Taylor promised to marry Billing 'if the sacred ties which bound them both to others should be dissolved'.

That was when the murder plot was hatched. Billing asked for Frarey's help to murder Mary, and in return she would help Frarey get rid of her husband, Robert. In August 1835 Billing and Frarey were indicted first for the murder of Mary Taylor and secondly for the murder of Robert Frarey – though chronologically Robert was the first of the two to die.

James Billing had an attack of cholera in February 1835 but recovered within four days – however, at the trial, it was hinted that the problem wasn't cholera. It was arsenic poisoning, but Frances hadn't made the dose strong enough to kill her husband.

The first murder, on 21 February 1835, seems to have been accidental. Forty-year-old Frarey was a childminder, and Harriet Southgate, one of the children she looked after, became ill very suddenly. Harriet's mother Elizabeth, a farm labourer, heard the news and rushed to the Frareys' house. She discovered that Robert Frarey was in bed, ill, with stomach pains, and baby Harriet was screaming. Elizabeth put some sugar in a cup of warm water and gave it to the baby – the age-old remedy for infant colic – and Harriet appeared to settle. But then, after a short sleep, Harriet went into convulsions and died in her mother's arms. Meanwhile Frarey made some gruel for her sick husband – and sweetened it with the same sugar.

Elizabeth Southgate gave evidence at the trial that Hannah died at Frarey's house and was buried from there. Robert Frarey was still ill; and

The pharmacy at Burnham Market where Billings and Frarey purchased the poison.

when Elizabeth called to collect her baby's clothes on afternoon of Wednesday 25 February she found that Robert had taken a turn for the worse. Billing came in with a jug of porter, apparently looking out for the Frareys as a good neighbour would. Billing said, 'Frary, [sic] I have brought you some porter but it has got warm on my counter.' She asked Catherine Frarey for a teacup, stirred the porter and poured some into a cup. Elizabeth noticed white undissolved powder in the porter. 'I couldn't drink porter with sugar in it,' she said. But Robert drank it anyway.

The truth about the sugar came out at the trial; it was laced with arsenic. Samuel Fuller Salmon, who worked for Mr Nash the chemist, served Frarey on 25 February with a pennyworth (a quarter of an ounce) of arsenic, which she said she wanted 'to poison mice with'. Billing was with her and asked for a pennyworth too. Salmon packaged the poison 'in separate white papers, with a label on each parcel.' He emphasised that the packages were 'double papered' and that the inner and outer papers were labelled with the word 'poison'. He noted that Frarey paid for both packages.

Later that evening, around 8 p.m., Elizabeth Southgate called in to see how Robert was doing. 'He was retching violently,' she reported. He asked her to hold his head while he was sick, and she noticed 'what came from his stomach was like water'. He was still ill on the Thursday evening; on Friday 27 February at 7 a.m. Elizabeth called in and discovered that Robert couldn't speak. She stayed for a couple of hours, when he became very restless. When she called in around lunchtime his mother and sister were there, along with Billing. Robert's eyesight was fading in and out, and finally he died in the afternoon.

Meanwhile, Robert's sister-in-law Sarah was ill at nearby Burnham Overy – and she died with very similar symptoms. Tongues began wagging, and rumours of poison where whispered throughout the village.

Elizabeth Southgate went to Wells with Frarey; on their return, she said, 'If I was you, Mrs Frarey, I would have my husband taken up and examined to shut the world's mouth.' Frarey, clearly knowing what would be found in any post mortem, disputed it. 'I should not like it, by no means, should you?' Elizabeth said firmly, 'Yes, I would like it; for if you don't it will be a check upon you, and your children after you.'

Frarey resisted the idea of a post mortem. And then the second part of the plan was put into place. On Saturday 7 March, Billing asked Jane Dixon to go with her to Mr Nash's for tuppence-worth of arsenic for Mrs Webster (the wife of a confectioner) of Creek [sic]. 'She wished me to go because it was not a rule to sell arsenic without a witness,' said Jane. So she accompanied Billing to the chemist's shop. Billing asked Henry Nash for tuppence-worth of arsenic, and he testified that she's said it was for Mrs Webster, 'who was very much over-run with mice and rats.' On the stand, Ann Webster swore that she'd never asked Billing to get her any arsenic. Nash wasn't to know that at the time, and Billing had the required witness with her, so he gave her the arsenic, plus a pennyworth for herself, a pennyworth of pills and a pennyworth of lemon drops. The arsenic, pills and drops were all put in separate papers and the Nash explained that he'd labelled the paper of arsenic as 'arsenic poison'. Billing paid for the purchases, then gave Jane Dixon a penny for her trouble in going with her.

Robert Loose, a shoemaker in Burnham Westgate, testified that the affair between Billing and Taylor was still going on; on a bright moonlit night just before Mary died, he saw them together near the Rose and Crown in pub Burnham. 'They were quite close together,' he said.

On 12 March, Mary went to work as usual. She'd left some Norfolk dumplings and some pork for Peter to warm up for dinner – but when she ate them she was violently ill. Peter, too, was sick. And Elizabeth

Southgate had seen Billing give a paper to Peter, that morning: clearly Peter had added the arsenic to the dumplings and eaten just enough himself to make it look as if he was innocent.

Frarey did the neighbourly thing and made some gruel to help Mary feel better – but Edward Sparks, a labourer from Burnham Westgate, saw her make the gruel. He testified that she 'took a small packet out of her pocket and poured the contents into the teacup and stirred it up'. The paper itself was white, and Frarey burned it on the fire; and the contents looked 'like powdered sugar'. This was white arsenic.

Later that evening, around 8.30 p.m.,William Powell, the blacksmith at Burnham Market, went to see Taylor to have his hair cut. He testified that Frarey was there with 'a pannikin of gruel' – all seeming kindly enough, though he noticed that she unfolded a couple of papers. She took a quarter of a teaspoonful of something that looked like powdered lump sugar, and three-quarters of a teaspoonful of something that looked like salt, put it on the tip of a knife and stirred it into the gruel. Billing came in to see how Mary was, and Frarey said, 'She's very ill, but the man will do.' She added that she was making gruel for Mary and intended to sit with Taylor 'and keep him company in his lonesomeness for an hour or two'. When Mary had eaten 'a considerable quantity' of the gruel, Frarey took the remainder into her own house, accompanied by Billing.

Phoebe Taylor had heard the news that her sister-in-law Mary Taylor was unwell, so she went to Mary's house in Burnham to see how Mary was. She found her sister-in-law 'sitting in a chair by the bedside, retching', calling out for water and saying that her stomach was on fire. Mary mentioned the gruel that Frarey had made for her, so Phoebe went next door, found the pan of gruel, warmed it up and brought it to Mary – but because Mary's throat was blistered by then, the gruel was too thick for her to swallow it. Phoebe put the pan of gruel on a chair, and Frarey came in and took it downstairs to water it down. She returned and gave it to Mary, saying, 'I hope, my dear, you'll take some of it now from me, and that it will do you all the good I wish.'

Taylor called Phoebe downstairs; Phoebe kept popping up to see Mary, but then she saw Mary in bed 'with her clothes laid' and Frarey was there with Mary Lake. Taylor asked Frarey to fetch Mr Cremer, the surgeon, but Frarey said it would do no good because Mary was too far gone. Taylor said he was too ill to go himself and begged her to go. Phoebe followed Frarey to Albert Cremer's house; but by the time the doctor arrived Mary was near the end. Cremer testified that he saw Mary in bed and alive, but her pulse was feeble and she was clearly dying. She died a few minutes later, so he stayed with her until her brother came.

Phoebe stayed with Frarey, Mrs Billing, Mrs Mills and Mary Lake, who 'laid out' Mary's body. Mrs Mills made them all some sugared tea (*The Times* referred to it as 'copious streams of tea'). But the condition of Mary's body excited suspicion, and Albert Cremer was called back to see the body and examine it for the coroner.

Francis Harrington Church, a surgeon who lived at Burnham Westgate, accompanied Cremer to the Taylors' house. He opened the body and noticed inflammation on the external coating of the stomach and part of the bowels: he suspected poisoning, so he removed the stomach and its contents and took them to the chemist Henry Nash for testing.

Meanwhile, on 15 March, Frances Billing had prepared a special dumpling for her husband. It was waiting for him by the fire when he came in – but he didn't fancy it and refused to eat it. Frances complained about it but eventually threw the dumpling away.

Nash confirmed that Church and Cremer had taken a stomach to him on 16 March for testing. Nash did two of the standard chemical tests: firstly with nitrate of silver with ammonia, which gave a yellow precipitate, and secondly with sulphate of copper with ammonia, which gave a green precipitate: both indicated that arsenic was present. Church took part of the stomach to the surgeon Richard Griffin in Norwich, who produced arsenic metal from the contents of the stomach.

The coroner, Mr Hammond, asked Church to search Billing's house. He found a swill tub in the outhouse that had flour on the sides. Then he went to 'the necessary house, which was common to the three houses'; he explained that 'the contents can be let out by a hole'. He did precisely this and found something that looked like dumplings or bread – the dumpling that Frances had thrown away, a couple of days before.

Church suspected that Billing and Frarey had poisoned some food and tried to get rid of the evidence. He cleaned the dumpling mixture and boiled it in glass vessel; then he subjected it to chemical tests with 'ammoniacal nitrate of silver', and the yellow precipitate that resulted suggested the presence of arsenic. Richard Griffin managed to produce metallic arsenic from the dumplings, too.

On the day of the inquest, Elizabeth Ward went to the Taylors' house to speak to Peter, and his neighbours Mrs Lake and Frarey came in. Fraey said, 'There you are, Taylor, we should both have been done if it had not been for our mother, God bless her: the gruel was boiled in mother's house.' Frarey apparently used to call Mrs Lake 'mother', even though they weren't related and Frarey was her lodger.

Billing was taken into custody at Walsingham Gaol; that day, Frarey begged Billing's son Joseph to hire a horse and gig and drive her to Salle, to see a woman who was 'something of a witch'. Her reasoning was that the witch would 'tie' the tongue of the gaolkeeper, Mr Curtis, 'so that he might not question my mother' (i.e. Mrs Lake).

John Claxton saw Frarey when Peter taken was into custody and heard her say, 'There you go, Peter, hold your own and they can't hurt you.'

The story of the porter and Robert Frary's death raced round the village; the body was exhumed, and on 27 March Francis Church examined the body. Although it had been buried for three weeks, he was able to do the chemical tests: and the results showed the presence of arsenic.

Billing confessed to the murder of Mary, though she said that Frarey had been the one to administer the poison. She also said that they'd had several other victims in mind – including her husband, Jim. He'd had an attack of 'cholera' not long before Robert Frarey was poisoned; now, it was obvious that it been arsenic poisoning, but Billing had misjudged the dose and not given him enough to kill. Billing said that she'd tried to kill him before, but then Mary Wright was 'taken up' for poisoning her husband, and what happened to her made Billing nervous of trying to do the same thing.

However, they weren't tried at the spring assizes as Frarey claimed to be pregnant. When this proved not to be the case, the trial went ahead at the summer assizes. Billing and Frarey said nothing in their defence on either count. Hannah Shorten was at the trial 'in custody for want of sureties to give evidence' and claimed that she wasn't a cunning woman. She said she wasn't the only one in Wells to tell fortunes, couldn't produce a love charm and never said she could, and simply told by the cards that there would be fatigue and trouble.

The judge summed up and reminded the jury to 'ignore the rumours' – meaning the accusations of witchcraft. The jury returned a verdict of guilty on both counts, and the judge passed the death sentence. At this point, Billing remained calm but Frarey went into hysterics; *The Times* reported that in 'the auditory' (i.e. those present at the court),'no sympathy appeared to be felt towards these monsters in human form'.

Though Billing at least had some sympathy at the end; her husband

and one of her sons visited her in her cell, and she begged James to forgive her, saying that he had always been a kind, indulgent and most excellent husband and father. James did indeed forgive her.

The *Norwich Mercury* printed the confessions of the Burnham Poisoners. Frarey confessed that she'd already attempted to poison Robert before she knew Billing; and Billing admitted that she'd mixed arsenic with Robert's pills and then put four more doses in tea and porter. She also confessed to putting arsenic in the gravy, flour and sugar in the Taylors' house, and said Frarey had put more arsenic in the gruel.

Billing and Frarey were executed on Monday 10 August 1835 in front of a huge crowd; *The Times* reported that there were over 20,000 spectators, and more than half of them were women. Although the hangman's drop was usually at the foot of the bridge over the castle ditches, the *Norwich Mercury* stated that it had been moved to the summit of the bridge 'out of pity to the women whose exhausted state might incapacitate them for a long procession'. Even so, Frarey needed support from the gaol to the platform.

At midday it was all over.

Though not quite for Peter Taylor. In the furore surrounding the case, he hadn't been tried. He'd watched Catherine Frarey and Frances Billing's execution and 'expressed a satisfaction at witnessing the shocking exhibition'. Then someone in the crowd realised he was there – and

Death masks of Frances Billings and Peter Taylor on display at Norwich Castle.

suddenly there were plenty of people who wanted to attack him for his part in the proceedings.

Taylor managed to escape and went back to Burnham. The villagers didn't want him there; they broke into his brother's house, smashing windows to get to him. He'd meanwhile hidden in a closet with a bedstead in front of it, so eluded their search; not for that long, though, because at the next set of assizes, in April 1836, he was indicted as an accessory before the fact to murder of his wife Mary. He claimed he was completely innocent and didn't even know what arsenic was – though nobody on the jury believed him. Quite apart from the fact that two years previously there had been a high-profile case in the nearby village of Wighton, when Mary Wright poisoned her husband with arsenic, arsenic was one of the most common rat-poisons used at the time. Taylor tried a different excuse, claiming that he'd been ill with rheumatic fever before his wife was ill, and he'd thought her illness was due to the fact that their meal had contained too many onions that day. Their neighbour Frarey offered them both gruel to help with their sickness and he accepted it, not knowing what was in it.

The jury thought otherwise. Particularly when witness Edward Sparks took the stand and said that on the day of Mary's death he'd seen Billing put her arms out of the window to give a signal, then he'd overheard a conversation between Billing and Taylor. The so-called innocent husband said, 'Never mind, she'll soon be done away with and then it will be all right with us.'

After a trial lasting eleven hours, the jury returned a verdict of 'guilty'. Taylor was sentenced to death and executed on 23 April 1836, still protesting his innocence.

The Hempnall Poisoner:

CHARLES DAINES, 1839

The case of Charles Daines is unusual because he was indicted on two separate days, on two separate counts – and the evidence was substantially the same in both cases. His defence team tried to argue that it was unfair as the charge was the same, and the law said 'no man shall stand in peril of life or limb more than once on the same charge'. However, the prosecution's argument was that the charges weren't the same – especially as the most important witness for the second case couldn't testify in the first case…

On Thursday 11 April 1839, 50-year-old carpenter Charles Daines was indicted for the unlawful murder of his own child, Elizabeth Daines, by administering to her a quantity of arsenic.

The trial began at 9 a.m. and witnesses unfolded events for the jury, starting from Sunday 10 March, 1839. Eighteen-year-old John Daines (Charles' son) testified that he came home at 9 p.m. on the Sunday night. His mother, Hannah Daines, was already upstairs and his father was in bed, so John locked the door after him. He then had a drink of water, using the pint mug that was kept on the washing stool. He explained that there was a pantry in the kitchen, and the tea kettle was kept on a shelf in the 'backhouse'.

On the Monday morning Daines rose early, as usual, lit the fire and put a kettle full of water on it. John and Hannah came downstairs; as was their custom, John and his father put their breakfast in a bag to take to work. Daines left to go to work at Mr Thirkettle's; John had a drink of water from the pail, using the same pint mug he'd used the night before, then left the house at 5.45 to join his father.

Hannah went about her usual morning routine; she tidied up and laid the breakfast things for herself and the two youngest children, then went upstairs and got six-year-old Edward and three-year-old Elizabeth dressed. They came downstairs and she brewed herself some tea, and made some 'sop' for the children with bread and water. Just as they were about to start breakfasting, her friend Elizabeth Mills called in, and Hannah invited her to stay. She put more tea in the teapot, and they began to eat and drink.

Within about two minutes, the children complained there was a 'hot taste' in their soaked bread. Hannah and Mrs Mills agreed that their tea tasted 'hot', too, but they continued eating.

Two minutes later, Elizabeth Daines let out a shriek and was violently sick. Hannah panicked and ran to her neighbour, Mary Alexander, and asked her to fetch Charles. John testified that at around 8 o'clock a girl called Fryer came to the shop with a message that Mrs Daines was very ill. Daines went home immediately, but John stayed at work until around midday.

Before Hannah Daines could make it home, she was sick; she couldn't walk without help. Mary Alexander led her back to her kitchen door, where they saw Mrs Mills and the children lying on the floor, shrieking in pain.

'The children were very ill,' said Mary. 'They reached much but could get nothing up. Elizabeth Mills was also there, very ill.'

The news flashed round the village that the whole family had been poisoned. Various neighbours went straight to the Daines' house to see what they could do and found Hannah, the children and Elizabeth Mills 'all labouring under the effects of some deadly poison'.

At this point, Daines reached home and turned to Mary Alexander. 'Are Elizabeth and Edward ill?'

'Yes,' she replied.

'Upon enquiry', according to Mary's testimony, Daines discovered that the tea and sop had been made with the water he'd put into the kettle over the fire. 'Surely there can't be anything in the water,' he said, adding that his son had been the last one up on the previous night and had drunk water from the pail. He took the kettle – an old one, according to Mary – from the fireplace and went outside. He poured out the water, rinsed it and refilled it from the beck (brook) with a fresh supply of water, and then set it on the fire.

Then he pointed at the sop. 'Have the children eaten it?'

He was told that yes, they had.

'Then I'll throw that away, too.' He picked up the dishes.

'No,' said Mary Alexander. 'Better let it abide until the doctor comes.'

Daines put the dishes down again without comment.

He clearly realised that the neighbours were starting to suspect him, because he went into the backhouse and came back with a broken basin full of a whitish-brown powder. 'This is poison for the mice,' he said. 'I don't know how any of it could have got into the water, unless the mice had been into the basin and then scraped it into the mug or the pail of water.'

The suggestion received short shrift from one of the neighbours. 'This would be a comical thing indeed: for who ever heard of a mouse getting into a pint mug!'

Someone suggested going for the doctor. Sarah Fryer, another neighbour who'd gone to the house because

Hempnall Street where Daines went for help.

she'd heard that Hannah was ill, said to Daines, 'Go and get some castor oil and antimonial wine.' The emetic, she thought, would make Hannah, Mrs Mills and the children, get rid of the poison by sickness or diarrhoea. 'You'll need to send for the doctor as well,' she added.

Daines didn't answer her. 'I'm going to get some medicine from the grocer's,' he said, and went out to Mr Thirkettle's in Hempnall Street.

Eliza Thirkettle testified that Daines had indeed come to her shop and told her his wife and children were very ill. 'I want castor oil to carry the sickness down,' he said. 'You have to give me something because they're dying.' He told her to 'make haste'.

'You really should send for Mr Utting,' Mrs Thirkettle said.

Then she clearly had a nasty thought. 'Daines, you haven't laid any poison about for mice or anything?'

Daines paused for a moment. 'I've laid fig powder about.'

He went back to the house with castor oil and antimonial wine.

John came in at about quarter past twelve and discovered the house full of people. He was shocked to see his sister so sick. 'Before then, she'd been really well,' he told the jury.

Finally Daines sent for John Utting, the nearest surgeon, who lived at Long Stratton. Utting walked in to see Daines supporting the head of his apparently dying wife, who was on her bed; Mrs Mills was lying on the floor and the children were supported in the arms of neighbours, moaning. The neighbours – Mary Alexander, Sarah Fryer and Sarah Rackham – corroborated the evidence, and Sarah Fryer added that Daines seemed very attentive towards his wife.

Utting intended to give them medicines to counteract the poison. He told the court, 'I had prepared some vomits of what we call sulphate of zinc or white vitriol, a remedy where we want to cause a sudden vomit.' But when he examined the children, he saw 'from the ghastly appearance, the coldness of the flesh, the dullness of the eye, and the largeness of the pupil' that there was no hope for Elizabeth. 'When I held the eye to close the light it gave no reaction,' he said. He suspected that the poison was arsenic – suspicions that were confirmed when he asked Mrs Mills what her symptoms were.

At 1 p.m., an hour after Utting arrived, Eliabeth Daines died. Three hours later, so did Mrs Mills. Hannah Daines and Edward were still ill but Utting thought they were likely to survive.

He immediately collected the evidence: the teakettle in which the water had been boiled, the teapot, some cold remaining tea in a cup, the sop in a basin, and half the loaf from which it had been made. He took them all back to Norwich and tested them with ammoniacal sulphate of copper. This produced a precipitate with a colour known as Scheele's green, showing that arsenic was present. Utting said that after the tests, he realised everything except the bread contained arsenic, and added that the tea and sop held 'a considerable amount of poison'.

Utting explained to the court: 'Arsenic destroys life sooner than anything; excessive depression, the pulse becomes small, the countenance pallid, ghastly; arsenic has a peculiar effect on the human heart itself, the natural action is stopped by arsenic. It seems to abolish the power of speaking. Laudanum and opium torpidises, but not so intensely as arsenic.'

He did a post mortem on the child's body, with the assistance of Thomas Henry Barton, a fellow surgeon at Long Stratton. Although Utting was fairly sure that arsenic was to blame, he found no arsenic in the stomach of the child, though the stomach was inflamed and looked 'redder than natural', especially at the smaller end.

The Norwich chemist George Warren Watts Firth analysed the powder in the basin, and discovered that it contained a mixture of *nux vomica* and arsenic.

Sarah Fryer testified that she'd overheard Daines say to Utting that he'd bought tuppence-worth of fig power from Mrs Browne for killing mice. She'd later heard that he'd asked for arsenic, but didn't want to trouble a witness (most chemists would only sell arsenic to someone if they brought a witness), so he bought *nux vomica* (also known as fig powder) instead. John Daines confirmed that their house had a mouse problem, so it seemed that Daines had bought the poison for a genuine purpose.

So where did the arsenic come from? The Times shed light on this, explaining that arsenic was often added to *nux vomica*. This was 'a very common practice with low shopkeepers in country villages, arsenic being so much cheaper than *nux vomica*'.

The evidence showed that Elizabeth Daines was poisoned. But did the evidence show that her father was responsible? The judge admitted that he'd stopped a case earlier in the circuit when Miss Ricketts had been accused of administering poison to her mistress in milk, but it was shown that poison was left lying round the dairy. 'There is a too frequent but careless practice of putting poison to destroy vermin,' he said. That was certainly true in the Daines case: the bowl of poison was left openly in the pantry. Sidney Taylor, the defence lawyer, felt that there was a danger of prejudice in this case, because a child was involved. 'Is it likely a quiet hardworking man would become a murderer?' he asked the jury.

Character witnesses spoke up for Daines. John Elsing, the village constable, testified that he'd known Daines for sixteen years and

Hempnall church where Mrs Daines was buried.

described him as 'steady, attentive to business…a very feeling man towards his children'. The curate of Hempnall, Rev Robert Rolfe, agreed that Daines had a good character, as did local farmer Joseph Webb.

The judge summed up at 8 p.m., saying that there was no motive so malice aforethought couldn't be proved. Daines had rinsed the kettle and filled it to give warm water to the affected persons.

The jury retired for half an hour and acquitted him as there was 'no evidence of any motive on his part to commit a deed so diabolical'.

Daines was led off to prison for the night, and was brought to the bar again on the moring of 12

April 1839, this time indicted with administering poison to his wife Hannah Daynes on 11 March with intent of his malice aforethought to murder her. Although the defence protested that the charge was the same and he'd already been acquitted, the prosecution said that it wasn't: the first trial was for unlawful murder, and the second was administering poison with intent to murder. And the evidence wasn't quite the same, either; the previous day, Hannah Daines hadn't been able to testify against her husband because she was his wife, but she was able to testify against him on the count of trying to murder her as she was personally involved.

The additional evidence, according to the prosecution, would show that Daines had a motive to murder his wife. The previous day's evidence was run through again. And then Daines' motive was revealed: over the previous two years, he'd 'formed a criminal connection with a woman named Lloyd'.

Daines met Ann Lloyd at Whitsuntide 1837, when he was working in Keswick, several miles from his home. Because travelling between home and work would take too long, he lodged with Lloyd's brother, Jonathan Gook. Lloyd was a tailoress who kept house for her brother. Daines clearly fell in love with her, though Ann's testimony was somewhat garbled. On the one hand, she claimed that 'he had taken liberties with me' while he lodged with her brother, but on the other that 'he used to allow very great respect for me'. Daines told Lloyd that his wife was 'afflicted' and wouldn't last two months. He added that if his wife died, he'd like to have Ann Lloyd as his wife; he asked her to stay single and wait for him for three years.

Jonathan Gook, Lloyd's brother, testified that she kept house for him. He hadn't actually seen any improper conduct between his sister and the carpenter, but he'd heard rumours, so he told Daines to leave.

Lloyd continued that 'since last Michaelmas' (i.e. 1838) she'd 'taken up' with a Mr Hawkes and 'had shunned the prisoner's company all she ever could'. But six weeks before the attempted murder, she saw Daines at Tasburgh church; he told her his wife was unwell and wouldn't last the winter. This was the last time she saw him.

Under cross-examination, any credibility she had as a witness vanished: she admitted that she'd lied on oath before the coroner by denying that she'd ever had criminal intercourse with Daines.

Then came the moment the court had been waiting for: the testimony of Hannah Daines. The prosecution added that she was 'deeply affected and is still labouring under the effects of the poison'; Hannah claimed that she still had 'darting pains in my stomach and arms'. According to the *Norfolk Chronicle and Norwich Gazette*, she went into the witness box and could scarcely stand. A chair was brought for her and she sat with her back to Daines for a while until she'd calmed down.

She testified to the events leading up to the poisoning; and then she spoke about Ann Lloyd. Lloyd was a widow who lived at Tasburgh, three miles away from Hempnall; she'd visited the Daines' house. According to Hannah, 'My husband had known her for one and a half years. We have had words because he has been too sociable with her to my liking more than once... he did not behave to me so kind as he used to do.' She tackled Ann Lloyd about it in the Horse Shoes Pub in Tasburgh; she explained that if Daines continued carrying on this way, she would have to leave him and she would end up in the workhouse at Pulham.

Lloyd told the court that she remonstrated with Daines, saying 'he didn't have the love for his wife and children he should have, and he should think of them not of me' – but Daines simply said that he couldn't help it. She was also very angry with Daines when he interfered in her relationship with Hawkes, and said to Hannah, 'If he comes near me I will give it him as hot as he can sup it.'

Benjamin Garrard, the shopkeeper at Tasbugh, testified next. He said he'd known Daines for about six months, and Daines came to the shop roughly once a week. 'A month ago he asked me for Spanish Figs... later he told me his wife was very ill from eating fried potatoes.' Hannah had indeed been ill, and at the time Daines had blamed it on the copper of the frying pan.

Robert Wyatt said that Daines had worked with him for many years; two weeks before the attempted murder, Daines had hung up his basket and told Wyatt he was 'much uneasy in his mind, the further he tried the further he fared off; he was tempted to make off with himself or his wife and family'. Daines was clearly unhappy with his marriage; when his lover spurned him, it tipped him over the edge into trying to get rid of his wife.

After the thirteen-hour trial, the jury retired for an hour and a half; they returned a verdict of guilty, and Daines was sentenced to death.

Afterwards, Daines confessed that he'd thought of murder for many months. He'd tried twice before; the first time, he tried putting poison in some fried potatoes but then an accident stopped his wife eating them. The second time, he put poison in pea soup but again failed. He'd bought

Gallows broadside for Charles Daines. © Norfolk County Council Library and Information Service

the poison months before in Norwich, and had hidden the packet in the thatch of his workshop. According to the *Norfolk Chronicle and Norwich Gazette*, he tried to kill Ann Lloyd, too – he was angry because she said she wouldn't marry him, so he sprinkled some poison on some biscuits. Luckily for her, she didn't eat them.

Finally, he put a 'drachm' (about as much as would cover a sixpenny bit) of the arsenic and nux vomica into the kettle, and Hannah finally drank it; the remainder of the poison was found exactly where he'd said he'd hidden it, in the roof.

Daines repented in prison and, according to the *Norfolk Chronicle and Norwich Gazette*, 'even when his iron galled his ancles [sic] and caused them to swell, and to occasion him a considerable degree of inconvenience and pain, he forebore to complain because he said he richly deserved all that he suffered'. He saw Hannah, Edward and John before he died; again according to the *Norfolk Chronicle and Norwich Gazette*, he fell to his knees in the cell and asked Hannah for her forgiveness. To his surprise, she gave it. 'How can you forgive me who have been guilty of the greatest crime I could commit against you, and for which I deserve the hottest pains of the world to come?' he asked.

On 27 April 1839 the scaffold, as usual, was placed in the middle of the bridge leading to the castle, and Daines was executed in what the *Norfolk Chronicle and Norwich Gazette* called 'the presence of one of the largest concourses of people ever witnesses here; the greater part of whom were females'. The newspaper report noted that the 'strictest order and decorum was observed; even though it was market day and they were intermingled with the cattle'. And the following Sunday, Samuel Hobson wrote a sermon preached to the village congregation, entitled *Be sure your sin will find you out! The rise, progress and consequences of sin considered.*

Daines' sin had found him out. And the consequences were a trip to the gallows.

Careless and Wicked Conduct:
FANNY ALEXANDER, 1842

Three years after the Daines case, people were still leaving poison carelessly about, and the judge wearily commented that he'd seen cases like this one too many times already on the Assize circuit.

Frances Alexander (known as Fanny) was indicted on 13 January 1842 for intent to murder her husband Terrington through putting arsenic in his dumplings, and her case was heard at the Assizes on 7 April.

Fanny, aged 20, married labourer Terrington Alexander in Wretton, Norfolk, the week after Michaelmas 1841. They appeared to be happy until around Christmastime, when Terrington admitted that they began to fight.

At 8 p.m. on 13 January 1842 she made four light dumplings and served them up for dinner; she ate one and Terrington ate the other three. Then she went to see a neighbour, Spinks, where she was very sick. During her absence, Terrington became ill, and he grew worse in the night.

Early the next morning, the village constable, James Hubbard, went to their house to investigate what was going on. Terrington was still very sick and complained of burning heat and pain in his throat and stomach; Hubbard testified that Fanny was also 'somewhat indisposed'.

'How did it happen?' asked Hubbard.

'I do not know,' said Fanny, 'unless some arsenic had fallen from the shelf into the flour from which the dumplings were made.'

Hubbard looked on the shelf and saw a small quantity of white powder. Fanny claimed she didn't know how it could have got there – unless her little brother had been playing with the paper and had accidentally pulled some of it into the pan in which the dumplings were made, which stood under the shelf. She stated she'd eaten one dumpling and Terrington had eaten three, and they were both ill during the night.

The constable took the white powder and 'the matter which the prisoner and her husband had thrown off their stomachs' and gave them all to the village surgeon, Henry Charles Brown Steele. Steele called on her to see what she knew about the powder, and Fanny started crying.

Steele and the Norwich chemist George Firth 'subjected [the powder and the stomach contents] to the usual tests for arsenic'. Steele testified that the results showed 'a considerable amount in the stuff vomited up', and the powder on the shelf was 'pure arsenic'.

The evidence showed that Terrington had been given poison in dumplings made by Fanny. But if she'd deliberately put the poison in the food, what was her motive?

Fourteen-year-old Hannah Stannard testified that she, Fanny and James Tokeley were 'dropping wheat' (i.e. sowing it) in a field in Wretton about two weeks after the Alexanders had married. According to Hannah, Fanny said to Tokeley, 'I'll poison my husband and get another, for I'm tired of him.'

Terrington was called to give evidence and was sworn in. He said that he'd married Fanny the week after Michaelmas; although they hadn't been happy, there hadn't been any serious quarrels between them. He stated that he had no reason to believe his wife had 'been guilty of any impropriety with Tokeley' and their arguments had nothing to do with Tokeley at all.

Constable Hubbard said that 'for certain reasons' James Tokeley of Stoke Ferry could not give evidence; the judge didn't press him to elaborate on his statement but seemed happy to accept it. The surgeons who tested the dumplings added that there was as much arsenic in Fanny's dumplings as there was in Terrington's.

The judge didn't bother to call Fanny to make any defence, and said that the jury should acquit her. The prosecution team had been correct in bringing the case, because the law should always make a full inquiry into the surrounding circumstances of any cases concerning death or attempts on the life of someone. However, he added that a jury must not act on conjecture or suspicion; they should proceed with caution as well as vigilance.

The judge felt that in this case, Fanny also ate the poisoned food and had been ill. Of her own free will she'd told the constable where the arsenic was kept: so in the judge's view her life had been in danger and there was 'no reason to suppose she had any wish to destroy herself'. He couldn't say how the arsenic had been mixed with the flour, but there wasn't enough evidence to show that Fanny did it. He 'lamented' and 'censured earnestly' the 'common habit which persons in the humbler walks of life in this part of the country had of leaving that fatal poison carelessly about their houses', and he had seen many 'reprehensible instances of this careless and wicked conduct'.

Given this direction, the jury acquitted Fanny. The judge ordered her to be discharged; he recommended that she should accompany her husband home and 'to endeavour by every means in her power, to fulfil her marriage vow, by loving and living in dutiful obedience with him'.

✐ Very Wrong ✐ct:
SAMUEL HOWLETT, 1844

Samuel Howlett's case is a very sad one. The threat of village gossip made his lover Ellen Jervis bully him into doing something very dangerous – so dangerous that it ended in her death.

On Friday 29 March 1844, 18-year-old Samuel Howlett from West Acre was indicted for the wilful murder of 34-year-old widow Ellen Jervis (widow), by administering arsenic on 2 September 1843. Thomas Williamson was charged with counselling him to commit murder and abetting him in the commission of the murder.

In the summer of 1843, Howlett was a groom in the service of Mr Edward Sherringham, farmer of West Acre. Ellen Jervis was also in service of Mr Sherringham, but lived in a house with her children about a mile away from her master's residence.

On 2 September 1843 Deborah Howell, a neighbour of Ellen's mother Mrs Wilson, saw Howlett call at the house somewhere between 4 p.m. and 5 p.m. Later that evening, she saw one of the children running out of the house and calling for help. Mrs Howell went in and saw Ellen sitting

Church at West Acre where Howlett and Ellen Jervis lived.

by the door in agony, complaining of a burning pain in her stomach. She sent for the surgeon, and intended to get Ellen to bed for some rest. The surgeon arrived; between them, they helped Ellen into the cottage, but before they'd gone more than a couple of yards, Ellen fell down and died.

A few days later, Howlett was suspected and arrested. The village constable took him to gaol, and on the way Howlett made a full statement. He said that, a few days before her death, Ellen asked him to go to Castle Acre and ask Williamson to recommend a drug to procure miscarriage.

Procuring abortion was a serious criminal act at this time; a doctor could carry out an abortion for the sake of the mother's health (usually saving her life), but the legality of this was in some doubt. If the abortion was carried out after the 'quickening' (when the mother first feels the baby move – usually in the second trimester, at around 16-20 weeks in a first pregnancy and earlier in subsequent ones), it carried the death penalty; abortions carried out before then (as in this case) carried a lesser sentence.

Nevertheless, Howlett went to see Williamson, who gave him directions to make up a 'decoction' that would do the trick. Howlett gave the instructions to Ellen, who made it and tried it. A couple of days later, she told him that she'd taken the decoction but it hadn't worked. She asked him to see Williamson again and ask for something else.

Castle Acre where Howlett purchased arsenic.

Howlett did as she asked, and Williamson told him to buy arsenic and make it into pills with suet or lard, then ask Ellen to take a pill every night for several nights. Howlett reported back to Ellen, who told him that if he didn't get the arsenic, she would come to his bedside in the night and cut his throat. So Howlett duly bought threepence-worth of arsenic and gave it to Ellen with Williamson's instructions. He begged her not to take it and said that he would support the child rather than let her take the poison, even if it meant he had to go on just one meal a day to pay the maintenance. Ellen was horrified at the idea; she said that she would never be seen to have a child by him, as she was old enough to be his mother. Clearly in this case she'd take her chances with death rather than subject herself to village gossip.

Joshua Love, the surgeon, testified that he went to Mrs Wilson's cottage to attend Ellen Jervis; she was sitting at the door and said she hadn't been feeling well for several days. He and Deborah Howell helped her into the house, but then she had a fainting fit and died. Love carried out a post mortem and found red patches on the coating of her stomach. This suggested arsenic poison; her stomach was empty, but he analysed the membrane and found arsenic. He also discovered that she was two months pregnant. He was, however, cautious about claiming the death was due to arsenic, as 'the tests were not infallible' and he hadn't been able to produce metallic arsenic.

When Williamson took the stand, he confessed to the abortifacient and arsenic remedies.

Justice Patteson summed up and told the jury that there was no evidence to prove that Ellen Jervis had taken the arsenic Howlett obtained for her. The only evidence of his guilt was his statement that he'd got it for her, and he'd also tried to dissuade her from taking it, so the jury couldn't find him guilty. If Howell was acquitted, then Williamson had to be acquitted too.

Both were acquitted and discharged for lack of evidence. *The Times* added that the 'learned judge' gave them both 'a very severe and impressive admonition'; the *Norfolk Chronicle and Norwich Gazette* reported it as:

You have down a very wrong act, I knew very well that one of you was persuaded by the woman to get some arsenic and the other was persuaded to give it; and I have not the least doubt it was to procure abortion; but perhaps neither of you had the least notion that she was putting her life in danger. Your object was, no doubt, to get rid of the child, and you procured the poison on her instigation, because she was ashamed of having a child by a person young enough to be her own son. Let this be a warning to you for the rest of your life.

Though Howlett and Williamson got off lightly. Only twelve years before, in March 1832, Henry Russell was indicted for murdering Mary Wormsley. Russell was the gaoler at the county gaol in Cambridge, and Mary was his servant. She became pregnant by him; he was shocked when he found out, said it was 'a bad job' and persuaded her to take some arsenic to 'procure an abortion'.

Before Mary died, she made a sworn statement to the magistrate's clerk, Mr Sweeting, explaining the circumstances, and 'put her mark to it'. Judge Vaughan said that the taking of arsenic by a woman to procure abortion might not be a felony in her case, but his opinion was that it was 'high misdemeanour'. Russell was found guilty of giving Mary Wormsley arsenic to produce a miscarriage but not of any intention to kill her. However, the judge still sentenced him to death, despite the protests of several of the jury.

Had Howlett and Williamson appeared before the same court, no doubt their sentence would have been the same.

The Happisburgh Poisonings:
JONATHAN BALLS, 1846

The story of the Happisburgh poisonings is truly shocking – partly because it involves a large number of murders over a long period of time, and partly because the village concerned, at the time, had a population of between two and three hundred people. As *The Times* commented, it is 'exceedingly strange that such deeds should have escaped the prying gossip of so small a village'. Particularly when it's possible that more than twenty people were involved. Why didn't anyone suspect what was going on? Or, if they did, why didn't they speak up sooner?

The tragedy of the case is that much of it could have been prevented. Magistrates had sent a circular to parish officers, telling them to make strict inquiries before they held an inquest because there had been complaints about the cost of coroners' inquests. As a result, John Pilgrim, the county coroner who lived in Chapelfield, Norwich, wouldn't start an enquiry until he'd had two or three requests. Had he investigated the first couple of deaths, it might have operated as a check on the poisoner. But it wasn't until the last three deaths that enough of a fuss was made to force an inquest. And, once the inquest opened, it was adjourned time and time again while more bodies were exhumed and tested, and more details of more unsuspected murders were revealed.

The enquiries revealed another, even sadder, layer beneath the poisonings: the case of Jonathan Balls' daughter, of an appallingly brutal marriage and the way it was all hushed up.

The whole thing came to light in May 1846. On 19 May *The Times* reported that people in Happisburgh 'have been in a state of great excitement in consequence of the exhumation of a number of bodies believed to be poisoned'. There were rumours that many people had been poisoned – Jonathan Balls, his wife and four grandchildren – so the county coroner, Mr Pilgrim, had to issue a warrant for the exhumation of various bodies.

Clearly this shocked the village the its surroundings; the bodies were placed in a tent at the back of the parish church, and *The Times* reported that hundreds of people collected round the tent. Mr Pilgrim had to

swear in a number of special
constables to preserve order
and 'prevent improper inter-
ference' with the bodies.
The enquiry into the
deaths of Jonathan Balls and
Elizabeth Pestle actually
started on Monday 11 May
1846 before Mr Pilgrim and
the jury at the Hill House pub
in Happisburgh (the pub
where Sir Arthur Conan
Doyle stayed and was
inspired to write the Sherlock

*The Hill House pub, Happisburgh where the
inquest into the poisonings was held.*

Holmes story 'The Dancing Men', published in 1903). Rumours of
poisoning were spreading all over the village; the vicar of Happisburgh,
Reverend Charles Birch, and the parish officers were anxious to have an
investigation. So the coroner duly swore in the jury and told them they
should ignore the rumours and look at the evidence.

Ann Pestle of Happisburgh – a 'decent-looking woman', according to
The Times – identified the body of her father, Jonathan Balls, and her
daughter, Elizabeth Pestle (her child). Her daughter had died on 15 April
1846 and her father had died five days later; both had suffered from
'violent vomiting and purging' but Ann didn't think it was anything to
do with poison. She thought her father had died of old age and her
daughter had died from a sore throat.

To modern ears, this is incredible: death from a sore throat? But infant
mortality in Victorian times was very high. There were major problems
with sanitation and public health, and houses were overcrowded, so
diseases such as cholera and typhus spread quickly. The Victorians had
large families but expected that few of their children would live to adult-
hood. So when children died, families mourned but the deaths weren't as
much of a shock as they would be to modern families.

Ann explained that baby Elizabeth was eight months old when she
died; she'd had 'something the matter with her throat' for the previous
nine weeks. Ann was a washerwoman by trade. 'When I went out
washing, I left the child with my father and my sister's little child,' she
said. Her father had lived with her for nine or ten weeks, but before that
he'd lived in another house a few hundred yards away in the village.

'When he lived in the village my girl frequently went to his house,' she said. And clearly she never suspected any ill-doing; she claimed that her father was 'always kind to children' and she'd never seen him 'with medicine'. When pressed, she admitted that her father sometimes went to Stalham (a larger village, four miles to the south of Happisburgh), but she'd never heard him mention a Mr Hockley (Thomas Hockley, the local chemist and druggist). She'd bought poison to get rid of rats, about twelve years before, but the poison had been used many years ago.

On 15 April, Ann came home from doing her washing work and found the baby very sick but unable to bring anything up. Elizabeth died a few hours later. On the Sunday morning before Jonathan's death, Ann testified that he'd eaten breakfast at eight, went out for a walk, then came back and complained of being numb and cold. He 'partook of a slight dinner', then an hour later went to bed. Clearly Balls was of a melodramatic turn of mind, because he asked for wine and some of Elizabeth's funeral cake; he claimed that 'death struck [him] in the morning in the yard.' He died a few hours later. He was seventy-seven years old, and Ann – clearly bewildered by the fuss and scared at having to stand before a jury – whispered that she thought he'd died from old age.

The inquest was adjourned so that the surgeons could examine the stomachs of Balls and Elizabeth Pestle. The jury saw Balls' remains – he had a walking stick on either side of his body in the coffin, an iron poker, several pocket-handkerchiefs and a piece of plum cake in each hand. It all seemed very strange: but the reasoning behind it wasn't explained until much later in the series of inquests.

At 9 a.m. on Thursday 14 May, the jury reassembled and the surgeons appeared before the court. William Clowes, the surgeon and registrar who lived at Stalham, deposed that on 20 April he was called in to see Mr Balls. Balls was vomiting and retching violently, complaining of great pain in his bowels and about the stomach. He died soon after, but at the time Clowes didn't think poison was involved; he merely thought that Balls had eaten some 'improper food'. However, after the inquest, he examined the body again, with the assistance of surgeon Mr Hewitt, who corroborated the evidence. The bodies of both Balls and his granddaughter seemed perfectly healthy and the surgeons noted the 'extraordinary preservation' of the bodies – a sign that made them suspect the presence of arsenic.

When they analysed Balls' stomach they found that it contained a large quantity of arsenic, 'undoubtedly' the cause of death. They examined the baby's stomach and it contained enough arsenic to kill her. George Warren Watts Firth, the surgeon from Norwich, examined the bodies too and said they had enough arsenic in them 'to poison the whole parish'.

Twenty-three-year-old Phoebe Ann Elizabeth Neave testified that she knew Jonathan Balls; she lived with her grandfather in the village and saw Balls once or twice a week. Two years before, he'd asked her to write a note for him to Mr Saddler, the 'chymist' at North Walsham, for some arsenic; Balls said he wanted it for destroying rats and he asked her because she'd previously written a note for his daughter Ann Pestle to the chemist for arsenic. Phoebe refused. 'I've heard of so many bad things being done with arsenic,' she explained. We can just imagine Balls' avuncular and slightly smile when he replied, 'Don't be afraid, I'm not going to use it for bad purposes.' Phoebe still refused to write the note; and no doubt, as the inquest continued, she was very glad that she'd stuck to her decision and hadn't unwittingly played a part in events.

The surgeon Mr Hewitt said that he had reason to believe all the exhumed bodies had been poisoned by arsenic. Reverend Birch was shocked; he said he hoped it would never happen again and he wanted a thorough investigation into what had really happened.

And then the political questions were raised; according to *The Times*, 'several gentlemen present' said that if the inquest had happened at the first death it might have 'operated as a check' on the murderer and saved several lives. They believed that the inquest hadn't taken place entirely because of the circular sent by the magistrates telling everyone to keep costs down.

The inquest was adjourned again so that the bodies of three other people could be examined.

On 20 May, the opinion of *The Times* was that there was 'very little doubt that the crime must have been going on for years, and it is hard to say how many persons have fallen sacrifice'. The article went on to describe the village as 'situate [sic] on a cliff overhanging the sea' and 'one of the most secluded villages along the coast'.

And the extra bodies?

The first ones to be exhumed were those of Jonathan Balls and Elizabeth Anne. But there had been several other deaths in the family in recent years. Jonathan was married to Ann Elizabeth Balls, who was six years older than him and had been bedridden for several years. They were both supported by parochial relief; the old man was 'not much liked in the village', and their three daughters were all married with children. Ann Elizabeth Pestle, aged 9 weeks, died in 1843 and was buried in the churchyard within a few hours of her death. Her brother Samuel died in similar circumstances in September 1845 and was interred next to his sister. The next to die was Ann Elizabeth, Balls' wife; because she'd been ill for a long time, nobody seemed to suspect anything. But when Elizabeth Pestle and then Balls himself died, rumours of poisoning began.

The parish authorities, mindful of the magistrates' notice about the cost of inquests, didn't send a notice to the coroner about any of the deaths. However, lots of people wrote to the coroner, to the point where he felt obliged to investigate. The first exhumations were those of Balls and Elizabeth Pestle; the next bodies to be exhumed were Ann Elizabeth Pestle, Samuel Pestle, and Ann Elizabeth Balls.

When the inquest began again, the first to make a deposition was William Pestle, Ann's husband. He explained that he was the father of Elizabeth Anne and the son-in-law of balls. He was a teamsman to Mr Storey – this meant his job was to look after the horses, and he was therefore employed throughout the year rather than as a labourer, who might be employed on a daily basis during busy times of the agricultural year. Certainly his day was a long one, as he said he was only home at night, from 9 p.m. to 4 a.m.

He told the jury that he had seen the three exhumed bodies, and confirmed they were his mother-in-law Elizabeth Balls, and his children Ann Elizabeth Pestle and Samuel Pestle. His mother-in-law had been dead for about nineteen weeks. William explained that he'd attended her funeral but wasn't there at the moment when she died, although he'd seen her a few hours beforehand. At the time of Mrs Balls' death, his wife Ann was there, together with her sisters Mary Green and Eliza Peggs; also with them were their neighbour Mary Slaughter, the Balls' servant Sarah Kerrison, and Jonathan Balls himself.

William explained that he lived about two furlongs away from Jonathan and Ann Balls (440 yards or roughly 400 metres) and saw them frequently. The coroner asked if he knew anything about what they'd taken.

'I know nothing about *that*,' said William.

The coroner asked him to explain what he meant by 'that', and William said he didn't know about the poison Jonathan and Ann were said to have taken. His wife had bought some poison thirteen or fourteen years ago when they had 'bad rats'; at the time William was working for Mr Pye, who recommended poison as the best thing for killing rats. So Ann Pestle sent a note with a little girl to get the poison. William never actually saw the poison in the house; as far as he was aware, his wife had laid it for rats in the coal hole.

But when William was pressed, he admitted that a fortnight previously (that is, about a week after Balls' death) John Wright, the local joiner, told him that Balls had been to Mr Hockley, the druggist at Stalham, and bought arsenic to kill some rats. William didn't know for certain that the house was infested with rats but had heard Balls say there were some, and Mr Pye, the local farm steward, showed him some rats in the barn that had been poisoned. William stated that he hadn't seen any poison in Balls' house; although he'd searched the house and Balls' clothes thoroughly, he'd found no trace of arsenic. He also said that he'd never heard his wife quarrel with her father and they were on good terms.

As for his children dying suddenly: he'd thought it a bit strange, but had never suspected poison. In accordance with his wife, he'd thought that their daughter had died from a sore throat. He added, 'My boy Samuel was subject to stoppages,' (probably fits) and he thought that was the cause of his death. One of the jurors interjected here to say that he'd seen Samuel when he'd had a 'stoppage' and confirmed that everyone else thought the same as Mr Pestle: that the death was from natural causes.

William was allowed to stand down, and Sarah Kerrison was called to testify next. Sarah was a servant who lived at Great Yarmouth servant and worked for Miss Lincoln in the Broad Row; she'd been born in Happisburgh and said she'd lived with Mrs Balls for nearly 5 years until she died. 'It was my duty to attend upon her,' Sarah explained, 'and I also attended upon Samuel, who was a dumb boy.' She painted a picture of Ann's life: 'She was very feeble, could not attend upon herself... I saw [Jonathan Balls] give her drinks, usually cold tea or water. He made tea in a teapot and poured it into another only used by her and she drank it through the spout.' (In Great Yarmouth's Tide and Time museum, there is an exhibit of an invalid cup, which looks exactly like a tiny teapot with a long spout.) Sarah said that Jonathan Balls was there as much as she was, and was always kind to his wife in her presence; the surgeon Mr Clowes attended Ann occasionally.

On the Friday before her death, Ann was very sick and 'discharged her stomach'. The following day, Sarah saw Balls put some water into the teapot and add a couple of pinches of white powder. She said it looked like flour. Although she didn't know where he got it from, she wasn't suspicious as she thought it was probably something to do his wife good.

The *Norwich Mercury* report of the inquest differs slightly here: it claims that Sarah said that when Balls put the white powder in the teapot, he did it as if he didn't want to be seen, but she was very sick at the time (from eating a poisoned kipper) so she didn't see where he got the powder from.

Ann Balls was sick afterwards and Sarah attended her until her death. Ann's three daughters – Mrs Pestle, Mrs Green and Mrs Peggs – were all with her on the Friday night and during the Saturday, but only Balls was there when Sarah saw the white powder going into the teapot. According to Sarah, Ann's daughters 'did but very little for her; they did not understand her ways'; however, Ann was fond of them and they were fond of her.

Sarah had no knowledge of any poison being kept in the house. But on the Saturday, Mrs Green was taken ill; she'd eaten a herring for breakfast and thought it had made her ill. Sarah herself was 'taken very ill' that night, although she couldn't remember what she'd eaten that might have made her ill. Balls said, 'I suppose we are all going to be taken alike.'

Sarah then took tea with Mrs Green and Balls, and they asked her what she thought off Ann Balls. 'I said he had had a deal of trouble with her, and that she did not appear to be a dying woman.'

Balls' response: 'Oh, I don't know that.'

In hindsight, Sarah said that 'he didn't seem hurt at her condition'. She added, 'I have heard he was spiteful.'

Mary Suffing, who wasn't related to Balls or his family but 'lived in the same yard', said that Mrs Balls 'looked sick, but I didn't think she was dying.' She too had 'heard nothing about poison'. But she clearly didn't like Balls, because 'he had low conversation.'

On the Monday night, Balls asked Sarah to get some water for Ann, because 'there was no telling what would happen in the night'.

Mary Slaughter, who shared a house with the Pestles, described Ann's last night. 'I was not with her when she was taken ill, but I was with her all the night she died. He was strange in his manner. He told me to take her pillow away from her head before she had expired.' Clearly she was unimpressed with Balls' behaviour. 'I said there was plenty of time for that. He asked if he should go and get the bell "passed" [tolled)].'

Phoebe Anne Neave again told the story about how Balls had asked her to write a letter to Mr Sadler for arsenic to get rid of the rats. 'When I refused, he said, "Why can't you write one for me as well as for my daughter, Mrs Pestle?" I told him it was twelve years ago and I was young then and knew no better.'

Ann Pestle wasn't the suspect for the murders. Reverend Charles Birch made that very clear when he said that Balls was 'a very singular and cunning man' and the vicar had never had a good opinion of him. Nobody suspected William Pestle either, as he had 'conducted himself and his family with every propriety' – and his wife was obviously included in that statement.

Mary Slaughter testified to what had happened to the other members of the family. 'I knew Balls, his wife and the grandchildren and attended them when they were ill. The whole of them were sick a few hours before they died. The little girl, Ann Elizabeth, aged nine weeks, died first. She had been ailing and was wasted away; she died in my arms. Her grandfather came frequently to the house after it was dead and said it was a happy release.'

By now, the jury were beginning to realise exactly what had been going on.

'Samuel was next,' continued Mary. 'He was taken ill at his grandfather's, who brought him home to his father's. He was taken ill at 5 p.m. and died at 8 p.m. that night.'

So was there a motive?

'I have known Balls ask for money and heard Pestle say he had lent money to him when he'd wanted it himself,' said Mary.

She also shed light on Balls' strange appearance in the coffin. 'The reason things were put into Balls' coffin is because he requested it to be done. I heard him say just before he died that as he had good things when alive he should like to have them when dead. He asked that a piece of plum cake was put in his coffin and his old woman's handkerchief put with his body.'

The next death was that of Balls' wife; then it was Elizabeth Anne's turn. 'I saw her just before she died. She'd been sick and I saw mucus on the bedclothes,' Mary explained. And at the child's funeral, she saw Balls drinking wine. 'He said it was the last glass he would ever have.' The night before Balls died, he told Mary's husband, 'I shall be dead before morning.' He added that he had had a good night and had made peace with his God.

Quite just how much peace he needed to make was still to be revealed.

Mary added that a child of Mrs Green's (Martha) had died suddenly some years before at East Ruston shortly after visiting Balls; an inquest had been held, but there was no post mortem.

Then came the surgeon's evidence. George Warren Watts Firth from Norwich said that baby Anne's body was badly decomposed so he couldn't trace any poison, but she may well have died from poison. Sam's body was very well preserved, and there were ulcers in the boy's stomach which were covered with brilliant yellow matter Firth suspected was a decomposition of white arsenic. He cut out one of the yellow spots and tested it, and arsenic was produced. Ann Balls' stomach was empty, but the coating of her stomach and part of her liver showed traces of arsenic; finding it in her liver showed that arsenic had been 'taken in a very large quantity'.

So far, there were five bodies: four of them had definitely died from arsenic poisoning, and the fifth was highly suspicious.

At this point the coroner called Balls' daughters: Mary Green, Ann Pestle and Eliza Peggs. He said he didn't know what turn the case would have taken, so he thought it best not to examine them on oath. He cautioned them that they could make a statement, but they didn't have to say anything that might 'criminate them' [sic].

The first to testify was Mary Green. She said that her daughter Martha had seemed fine except for a few blotches on her skin. She was busy at work getting 'hovers' (turf) up, so her mother took Martha to their house in the donkey cart. Mary went to collect her daughter on the Monday; her father met her and said that the little girl had died. Mary was shocked because Martha hadn't seemed that ill. 'Mr Clowes examined her but she wasn't cut up. We thought she'd died of fever. She was never very well. Three weeks before she died, she had a bad throat.'

The similarity with what had happened to Elizabeth Ann Pestle was only too clear.

But Martha wasn't the only child of the Greens who'd died. 'William died five years ago,' Mary explained. 'I had four others at home ill at the same time. He'd been living with my father for eighteen months and was coming back as my mother was going to move. He was taken ill the day before he came home and died three weeks later.' Poison hadn't even crossed Mary's mind.

Turning to recent events, she explained, 'Father wished us to have a herring for breakfast. Kerrison and I had one. We were taken very sick –

I was sick all night and Kerrison was sick for two days.' Clearly the herrings had had a very special seasoning. 'I never heard of anything being put in Mother's teapot.' At this point, the enormity of what her father had done – and how close Mary herself had been to death – clearly sank in, and the poor woman went into hysterics.

Robert Green, Mary's husband, testified that he'd been ill, the previous year; however, it was when he'd been in the workhouse so it couldn't have been Balls. He, like William Pestle, had trusted his father-in-law. 'I never thought Balls did something wrong but now I believe he did.'

The case took an even sadder turn, when Rosanna Peggs – Eliza's sister-in-law – testified. 'I thought it odd that Maria Green died so suddenly,' she said, referring to Mary's daughter who died in 1836. She added, 'Balls' daughter [Maria Lacey] died suddenly and her daughter too, twelve years ago. No inquest was held.' Though she admitted that there was lots of talk about the way Maria Lacey's husband behaved: 'He kicked her and used her badly.'

Mary Green was re-examined, and her testimony was heartbreaking. She agreed that her sister had been badly treated. 'Her husband beat her when she was confined. She couldn't walk without her hands on her body.' Not only was William Lacey a bully and a wife-beater, he was very mean: 'Her husband gave her five farthings a week.' It wasn't enough to keep the family, and Maria wasn't entitled to parish relief. Apparently, the neighbours were kind – but Lacey was completely unrepentant. 'He said if she got better he would use her worse than ever, and would not spend a farthing to bury her.' She added that Lacey was the cause of her sister's death. 'He is married again, and has four children.' In Lacey's defence, she said, 'He treated her well when they lived with my father but ill-used her when they went to live with his mother.' Jonathan Balls had promised to give Lacey some furniture for the house but didn't; perhaps Lacey took out his resentment on Maria. 'I didn't visit her there as I didn't like her mother-in-law,' Mary added.

According to the *Norwich Mercury*, one juror said it was hard to get people to talk about Lacey as they were afraid to speak.

Mary then spoke about her father's death. 'He said he was dying and I could leave him. I heard that on the day before he died, he came out of the garden and said death had struck him while he was at work. He was very sick and went to bed. He asked Mrs Pestle to give him some of the child's funeral cake and a glass of wine. He said it would be the very last he would take, and the remainder of the cake and wine would serve for his funeral.' He died at 8 a.m.

It turned out that Mrs Green had had eight children, all of whom were dead. 'Nine or ten years ago, one died in my father's house. It was very sick and died in two or three hours,' she stated. And she was obviously just beginning to realise why.

Eliza Peggs thought that her daughter had died from smallpox. A neighbour looked after her and her 6-year-old sister. Eliza herself had had a very bad illness before Maria Lacey died, and was very sick. 'My father never came to my house, although he was friendly with my husband. Only my mother came.' Then she gave some incredibly surprising evidece: 'My father lived with Lacey when my sister died.'

Balls must have heard the rumours. Given his habit of poisoning people, why hadn't he tried to protect his daughter by poisoning her husband before he beat her so badly?

The evidence given by neighbour Mrs Lawson is even more horrific. 'William Lacey is a fisherman. He has a violent temper when put up – he is a drinking man.' That would explain one of the reasons why he beat his wife. And worse: 'There was a mark on Maria Lacey's body like the toe of a shoe. Sarah Tuck the midwife and I were laying out the body. There were blisters which burst when we put the shroud on and bloody water came out.' Eliza Peggs admitted that her sister's body was badly swollen – and also that their mother had told Maria not to complain about her husband but put up with it.

Maria Lacey, as a woman with no money and no recourse to the courts, was helpless. It's clear that everyone in the family and the neighbours knew what was going on. But not a single person was able or willing to stop Lacey from lashing out at her. Clearly they were too frightened of William's temper to try to shelter her. And if she wouldn't testify against her husband (probably through fear), the local magistrate wouldn't be able to bind him over to keep the peace.

The one person who doesn't seem to have been afraid of anyone – Jonathan Balls – didn't help her… unless he thought that poisoning her was the only way to stop her pain. Given the evidence that unfolded later, that's very, very doubtful.

Whether Maria's death was due to her husband's brutality or poison wasn't clear at that point in the inquest. Mary Green stated that Maria had a child by Lacey before the marriage and another child after the wedding, which later died: this hints that both Maria and her child were the victims of Jonathan Balls.

The coroner summed up and said that no evidence pointed to any party – if anyone was to blame, it was Jonathan Balls, who was beyond the reach of the law. Half an hour later, the jury decided that the victims all 'died from the effects of poison, but how administered there was no evidence to show'.

But this wasn't the end of the matter.

On Monday 1 June, the case took another turn when the Secretary of State, James Graham, said that he intended to reinvestigate the circumstances of the deaths. A government officer, aided by the county's chief constable, Colonel Oaks, made private enquiries and discovered that the number of cases of poisoning was much higher than first thought.

The culprit was Balls, who got rid of his bedridden wife; although it was wrong, his motive was understandable because Ann Balls 'now and then occasioned him some trouble'. But the investigators didn't understand why he poisoned the children, as he didn't support them financially and usually showed kindness to them. Within twelve years, eight of Mrs Green's children and four of Mrs Pestle's children died after being attacked with similar symptoms – as did Jonathan and Ann Balls.

Several people testified that Balls was in the habit of buying arsenic, and procured it in many neighbourhoods. Some people in village remembered that Balls' mother and father came to live with him twenty-two years ago and shortly afterwards died 'very suddenly and in the same way as the others'.

But Balls didn't confine himself to poisoning his family. The investigators found that 'during the last few years many labouring men who were in the habit of mixing greatly in Balls' society, and visiting him at his house, have died after 2 or 3 days' illness and from a cause far from satisfactorily explained'. The constable added that 'Balls was in the habit of perpetrating disgusting offences' and had twice been charged with arson. He was 'generally termed in the village as a mischievous old man'.

Another reason Balls was the chief suspect was that Mrs Green kept the membrane her daughter threw up and said she was going to get the surgeon to examine it. Balls said, 'Oh, don't do that,' but she said she would – and a few hours later he was dead from poison. Clearly he killed himself to avoid the inquest and the trial that would clearly ensue.

During the inquest report at the Swan in Stalham, there was a rumour of even more deaths. Balls' son, also called Jonathan, died in mysterious circumstances; Mrs Sieley, the wife of a gentleman in the parish for whom Mrs Peggs did washing, also died in mysterious circumstances. Out of the next five bodies exhumed, two had definitely been poisoned – Maria Lacey and Maria Green. Mrs Peggs fainted when the coroner spoke of the death of Mrs Green's children. The coroner gave an open verdict, and the jury's verdict on Elizabeth Ann was that she died of fever.

Robert Green was clearly unable to take it in. 'I've lost eight children. Some were born dead. One died at Smallburgh.' We can almost hear the shock and disbelief and desperation in his voice as he said, 'Balls was always kind.' But, according to the *Norwich Mercury*, his wife was far less sanguine about it. 'If I'd known what my father did I would've hung him.'

The final inquest was held at the Butcher's Arms pub in East Ruston. The *Norwich Mercury* summed up the jury's verdict:

It was lamentable to perceive in what a state of wilful wickedness and ignorance many of the lower orders of society still remained... We all naturally wish to keep down the county expenses, but not at a sacrifice of human life... We think this case will operate as a caution to parishes gener-ally as to the necessity of investigation before coroners and surgeons, when there is the least suspicion all is not right.

Some commenters tried to blame the chemists for selling the poison to Balls in the first place: but with communications being what they were in the nineteenth century, and the fact that Balls was careful to buy his poison from many different places, it's unlikely that any of the chemists or druggists would have heard of the suspicious deaths.

And finally the verdict on Jonathan Balls himself was given: again, according to the *Norwich Mercury*, Balls' 'crimes appear to rival in enormity those attributed to Marchioness Brinvilliers and other "poison-ers" of the eighteenth century... Things are now related of him that would disgrace a savage and are utterly unfit for publication.'

Of course, this didn't stop the *Mercury* publishing them.

Apparently, twenty-six years previously, Balls burned down his own cottage to get sympathy and a 'subscription' from people (i.e. people gave money to buy him a new one – much as in the way that people can donate to disaster funds in this century). In 1830, two farmers' haystacks were burned in Happisburgh – Mr Howes and Mr Sieley. Then Balls tried cadging at farmhouses; Mr Cooke at Stalham refused to give him anything, and 'five minutes after he left, the tythe [sic] barn was discov-ered on fire'. Again, Balls was implicated; he met two women on the road shortly afterwards and said to them, 'Don't you see the fire?' The fire couldn't actually be seen from that point in the road – but by the time they'd realised that, he'd 'scarpered'.

Balls was a pauper – the *Mercury* said that 'no one would employ him in consequence of his disgraceful conduct'. Their view was that he was financially dependent on his daughters, so he poisoned their children to free up funds so they could support him better. Seven of Mary Green's children died suspiciously between 1836 and 1846; three of Ann Pestle's six children were poisoned and another died in suspicious circumstances; and one of Eliza Peggs' children died in suspicious circumstances. All of the children died at his home or soon after leaving it.

Of Balls' three sons, Robert lived at Scottow and would have nothing to do with his father. James and Jonathan died twelve years before 'in mysterious circumstances' and were buried at Catfield; the medical experts' view was that the bodies had been buried for so long that there probably wouldn't be a trace of arsenic left.

The full extent of the Happisburgh poisonings will never be known,

but they are likely to include several workmen and, within his family, Balls' mother and father, two of his sons, one of his daughters and her child, twelve of his remaining daughters' children, his wife, and finally himself. It's stunning to think that his family trusted him so much they didn't have the slightest clue that these sudden deaths were all suspicious. Or maybe it was an idea they found so shocking that they wilfully ignored it in the hope that it wasn't true.

Sadly, it was. And although Jonathan Balls is reputed to be buried in the grounds of Happisburgh church, it's in an unmarked grave.

Happisburgh church where Balls has an unmarked grave in the churchyard.

The Tibenham Poisonings:

BY PERSON OR PERSONS UNKNOWN, 1847

In March 1847, two sisters were poisoned by arsenic. There appeared to be no motive; village gossip had it that the maidservant was responsible, but there wasn't enough evidence to connect the arsenic with her.

The *Norfolk Chronicle and Norwich Gazette* reported the following week that local farmer Cain Small had been taken ill and died suddenly; the same day, Mrs Self, the wife of a local farmer, attended the market as usual at New Buckenham, was taken ill suddenly at the King's Head Inn and died. Was it the poisoner wreaking more havoc, or just a coincidence?

John Pilgrim, the coroner, opened the investigation at the Greyhound Inn in Tibenham on Tuesday 30 March 1847.

Joseph Pearson, husband of Mary, was the first to give evidence. He stated that they'd been married for over twenty years and had always lived in Tibenham. Mary was fifty-nine years old and had been in good health – he couldn't remember when she'd last been unwell.

On the morning of Sunday 28 March, they'd sat down to breakfast at 8 a.m. Their maidservant, Eliza Sage, and their 'lad', James Warren, sat

Greyhound pub, Tibenham, where the inquest into the murders was held.

down in the same room at a table near theirs. For breakfast, they had tea, bread and butter and cheese. Mary cut slices from a new loaf of bread made the previous morning, poured the tea, and drank it before she ate. She took two or three mouthfuls of dry bread, and said it had been made of old flour.

But Joseph was worried: 'I had discovered a difference in her countenance.' Worse, she couldn't get her breath. Mary said that the new bread didn't suit her stomach; she went out of the back door and 'discharged her stomach'. Then she came to sit by the fire, and Joseph sent for Horace Howard, the surgeon at New Buckenham. He also sent for his sister, Elizabeth Everett, to come and attend her. Elizabeth had some of the tea and was also 'sick and violently ill'. The doctor arrived somewhere between eleven o'clock and midday, and Mrs Pearson died shortly afterwards; at four o'clock, Mrs Everett died as well.

Joseph knew exactly where all the food on his table came from. 'The tea was purchased from a man who travels about the county, by the name of Peter Hurner. He lives in Yarmouth and we have had tea from him for many years.' He thought it unlikely that the tea was poisoned. 'The flour for the bread was made from wheat of our own growth and butter from our own making, and the cheese was bought from Mr West of Tibenham.' He added that he had bread and cheese but no tea; he'd had half a pint of beer with his breakfast instead. 'The servants and have I eaten the same bread, cheese, butter, milk and sugar, and we have not been ill.' The only different thing was the tea: 'Our girl didn't take tea; she has been having milk lately. I haven't drunk tea since.'

Sage the maidservant was the one who'd poured water from the kettle into the teapot. Could the problem have been with the water? 'We have no pump,' Joseph explained, 'so the water is taken from a pit near the house. Other people take water from there, too.' But there hadn't been any other reported cases of illness in the village.

'I can't account for the deaths,' said Joseph, clearly at a loss. 'My wife and sister were perfectly well. I was on good terms with my wife.'

And then the question of poison arose. 'My wife told me we had mice upstairs and she'd stopped the holes up with poison to destroy them,' Joseph said. 'This was last Thursday. I didn't see the poison and don't know where she got it.'

The maidservant, seventeen-year-old Eliza Sage, was next in front of the coroner. John Pilgrim warned her not to say anything, unless she pleased, that might 'criminate herself'.

Sage deposed that she'd been living with the Pearsons as their servant 'since Michaelmas', and corroborated Joseph's evidence. 'The mice were troublesome, so Mrs Pearson laid a great deal of poison on Thursday. I swept the closet at noon and put the dust on the fire. The kettle was not on the fire or near it at the time; it was in the wash-house.' Sage added, 'My mistress always behaved well to me.'

Thomas Everett, Joseph's brother-in-law, was next to give evidence. 'My wife was in good health. She was sent for to go to Mrs Pearson, so she went without having her breakfast. She came back and said Mrs Pearson was very bad. Then she left the room and I heard her scream in the privy. I went to her, and she was retching violently and casting up her stomach. I was with her for half an hour; she said she was dying. I carried her upstairs and gave her some brandy, but she got worse and died at 4 p.m.' He, too, was at a loss as to who'd administered the poison. 'I don't know who would do it.'

Horace Howard, the surgeon from New Buckenham, testified that he'd been sent for to attend Mrs Pearson and Mrs Everett. He couldn't account for either of their deaths.

John Pilgrim – perhaps mindful of the recent case in Happisburgh and wondering whether this was the start of another mass murder – said that Mrs Pearson and Mrs Everett were both 'much esteemed' in the neighbourhood; there must be a post mortem and an examination of the contents of the bodies. Mr Howard agreed but said he wanted Mr Firth to assist him.

The bodies hadn't been interred, so the jury viewed them; and the jurors were unanimous in wanting a full investigation. The inquest was adjourned until the examinations had been made.

On Thursday 8 April, the inquest resumed – still at the Greyhound in Tibenham. The coroner said that from what he'd heard, the poison must have been mixed in the tea kettle or in the teapot used at the meal.

Sage took the stand. She'd heard people say that she'd poisoned Mary Pearson; others in the village said that Joseph Pearson was the poisoner. She sounded aggrieved when she added that Joseph wouldn't let her go out as people would ask her questions. She said that on the Sunday night, John Pearson (Joseph's brother, also a farmer) and his wife came over; they asked her to pour water out of the kettle and check there wasn't a toad in there. They also told her to get an ounce of tea from their neighbour Mrs Warren, as they dared not drink any of the tea in the house.

Joseph Pearson had some new evidence to impart. 'The Wednesday after my wife's death. I was in Tibenham Street and heard my sister Mrs Everett and her son Thomas had had differences. Thomas said to his mother, "The sooner you are dead, the better, for she was the biggest old liar in the town," and said, "Do you want me to give this woman some poison?" She said, "God forbid, Thomas, that you should do that!"'

So could Thomas have been the murderer? It was unlikely, because it would have meant murdering his aunt first. Had the deaths been the other way round – with Mrs Pearson being called to attend Mrs Everett during sickness – then he would have been a more plausible suspect.

Joseph continued that on the Thursday after his wife's death he was at home; Mr and Mrs Filby, her sister-in-law Mrs Lincoln and his servant girl Eliza Sage were all present. His brother-in-law Thomas Everett came in, looked at Mrs Pearson's body, and then they all went to view Mrs Everett's body. Thomas, Joseph's nephew, was there when they went to the Everetts' house.

The next to give evidence was eighteen-year-old James Warren. 'I've been a servant to Joseph Pearson since last Michaelmas twelvemonth. I take my meals in the same room as them, only at another table. At dinner we sometimes dined at the same table and shared the same food. When we breakfasted on 28 March, I and Eliza Sage the maidservant were at another table. I had a basin of milk and a bowl of bread and cheese, and –' very tellingly '– Eliza Sage had none. I do not know why.'

The jury had a fairly good idea because they'd heard the rumours.

'I cannot say if my master had tea that morning,' Warren added. 'He always had beer, but sometimes I have seen him take tea.'

After their mistress's death, Warren admitted that he'd said to Sage, 'This was a bad job for me and her and others.' He clarified for the jury that he'd meant, 'I had lost a good mistress, and now she was dead she could do no more good for me.' He added that he'd never seen poison in the house, but he'd heard mistress talk about having laid poison in a cupboard for mice.

A couple of days later, Warren spoke to Mrs Everett's son John. 'It's a bad job for me, and what a wonderful thing it is.' It seems an odd word to use, and clearly the jury picked up on it, because he clarified that by 'wonderful', he'd meant it was surprising that the two deaths happened so quickly together.

John's reply was, 'I want my mother.' Clearly they'd had some sort of argument, because Warren claimed John Everett also said. 'I have not been so dutiful to her as she was to me. I little thought of death being so nigh. If I had, I should have behaved better.' Everett also told Warren that on the Saturday before she died, his mother had said to him, 'John, you will miss me when I am gone.'

By this point, the jury were becoming impatient because Warren's testimony wasn't leading anywhere. The conversations he reported weren't relevant: John Everett wasn't under suspicion and what he'd said could apply to just about any relationship between a parent and an adult child at some point.

Warren was clearly trying to cast suspicion on John Everett, because he said, 'I told him we'd have to go up before the jury at the inquest. John said we had to be sure to tell one tale and not stories. Then he said, "If we tell different tales, what a strange thing it will be."' Warren then claimed he hadn't talked to John Everett about the cause of his mother's death and had only spoken to Joseph Everett and Eliza Sage about the subject.

The coroner didn't believe him. 'It had been the talk of every house in the village so you couldn't have avoided talking about it. Who else spoke to you?'

Warren claimed he couldn't remember – someone asked if Mrs Everett had been poisoned but he couldn't think who.

The coroner and jury thought he wasn't telling the truth and was evading questions; just what was Warren hiding?

'Everyone in the village thought Mrs Everett had been poisoned,' Warren claimed. Then he slyly added, 'I don't know what Eliza Sage and John Everett thought. I saw them talking together.' But when pressed to say when, he couldn't remember if it was a month or a day 'since John last came by the house'.

His testimony then turned to the household arrangements for water. Warren couldn't recollect filling the kettle, but he brought the water from a pit at the side of the road. 'It's a running stream,' he added. He said that Eliza used to fill the kettle. She told him after their mistress died that she filled the kettle on the Sunday – but again his memory suddenly failed him, because he couldn't remember when or where she told him that.

By then, the local newspaper reporters were losing patience with Warren, too; the *Norfolk Chronicle and Norwich Gazette* said that Warren 'proceeded to give a long account of conversations with different persons that proved nothing'. The coroner ordered him to be taken in by the police.

Eliza Sage was called next. She deposed that she was the maidservant to Mrs Pearson, who was in good health until the day of her death. 'On that morning I filled the kettle for breakfast, from a pail. The kettle was in the copper hole. The Saturday niught before, Mr and Mrs Pearson had tea. I filled the kettle and got the water.' Her evidence then corroborated Warren's: 'The water was from a pit that is supplied by a running stream. I took the water from the pail in a cup to fill the kettle. It was the same water I used the next morning. There was some water left in the kettle on Saturday night, and it remained there all night. I didn't throw it out when I filled the kettle on Sunday morning. I don't take tea in the mornings and I didn't take it on Saturday night.'

Clearly the Pearsons weren't ill on the Saturday night, so the poison must have got into the kettle at some point between Saturday night and Sunday morning. Who might have put it there?

The coroner asked who else was in the house on Saturday night. Sage replied: 'Only the master, my mistress, myself and Warren.' She said she hadn't seen anyone else. 'And I must have seen them if they had been there, because I was in and out of room while Mr and Mrs Pearson were there.' She explained that Warren only drank milk, both night and morning. And she summarised the events on Sunday, as she saw them: 'When my mistress was taken ill, I went for Mrs Everett, who came immediately. Mrs Pearson asked her to have breakfast and she had two cups of tea and some bread and cheese. Mrs Everett stayed half an hour then left; as she was going home, she fell ill. Mrs Pearson died at twelve and Mrs Everett died at four.'

Had she talked to anyone about the deaths? 'No, not to anyone,' Sage said. 'My master wouldn't let me go out because people would ask me questions.' But she must have talked to *someone*. Then she admitted, 'The Sunday after she died, Warren said, "It was a solemn thing to see two people die on one day."'

The coroner's questions became more pointed. 'If there was poison in the tea kettle, how did it get there?'

'I have no idea,' said Sage. 'I am very sorry if that was the case, as my mistress was good to me.'

What happened to the water from the kettle?

'The doctor took away water that remained in the tea kettle on Sunday. I filled a bottle with the water from the kettle on the same morning, to warm my mistress's feet.' This, too, had been taken away for analysis.

When pressed about what had happened to the kettle on Saturday night, Sage answered: 'I put the kettle in the copper hole in the backhouse on Saturday night and put it on the fire on Sunday morning, before I went milking.'

And then there was the question of John Everett – what had she been saying to him when she'd been seen with him? 'I have not talked to John Everett since her death.'

And was it true that she got on well with her mistress? What about the arguments they'd had?

'When I first went into her service we had some angry words,' Sage admitted, 'but not lately.'

On the question of the mouse poison, she explained, 'On the Thursday before her death, my mistress took me up in her room and showed me some mice holes in a closet. She put poison in the holes – it was something mixed up in a basin. I swept out the closet and there were bits of poison in the dust, which she threw on the fire. There was no vessel on the fire when she threw the poison in the fire, and the kettle was not near it.'

Clearly the tea kettle had made the family nervous. 'On Sunday night Mrs John Pearson, her sister, called and directed me to fetch another kettle for tea, as she was afraid to drink out of the one that had formerly been in use.'

Then she admitted something odd: 'The medical gentlemen had the kettle that was boiled on Sunday morning. The wrong one was given to them at first but then the mistake was rectified.'

Who gave them the wrong kettle? Was it Sage, because she knew she'd put the poison in the kettle in the first place?

George Watts Warren Firth, the surgeon of Norwich, testified next. He said that on 31 March, along with Henry Howard of New Buckenham and his assistant, he performed the post mortem on the deceased. 'Mrs Mary Pearson was healthy. Her stomach contained 12 oz of yellow liquid, a little tinged with blood. The lining of her stomach was soft and yellow and there was some slight effusion of blood from the first small intestine.' These were signs of arsenic poisoning, as were his next observations: 'The brain and its membranes were loaded with blood.' Mrs Pearson wasn't as healthy as she looked, though. 'Her heart was small and weak, and there was some disease about the valves.' Firth performed a chemical analysis of the stomach contents and part of Mrs Pearson's liver, and obtained arsenic; he stated clearly, 'The cause of her death was arsenic.'

What about Elizabeth Everett? 'She looked healthy too. Her stomach was inflamed; there were more contents, the fluid was tinged with blood and there were pieces of cheese floating in it. Her brain's blood vessels were congested.' Nobody was surprised when he concluded, 'I analysed the stomach contents and her liver, and found arsenic in her liver.'

The constable at Tibenham, Frederick Bloomfield, had given Firth some other items for analyis. 'A tea kettle, water in a stone bottle, and some in a glass bottle.' He also examined the tea leaves 'and some greasy paste in a basin.' Unsurprisingly, arsenic was present in all of them. 'The kettle had small a trace and the glass bottle had a small portion of arsenic. The stone bottle had most and was clearly not the same sample.'

Sage had already admitted to filling the stone bottle with the same water used to make the tea drunk by Mrs Pearson and Mrs Everett. She'd also given the medical examiners the wrong kettle. Had that given her the chance to wash out the kettle, so there wouldn't be quite so much in it?

Horace Howard, the surgeon of New Buckenham, confirmed that he'd been called to the deceased on 28 March between 11 and 12 in the morning. 'Mrs Everett was collapsed and in a sinking state, and Mrs Pearson was insensible and dying.' He also corroborated Firth's evidence of the post mortem and chemical analysis.

Frederick Bloomfield, the constable of Tibenham, deposed that he found the kettle, the stone and glass bottles, the water and the greasy paste at Mrs Pearson's house. Firth added that he hadn't seen any of the greasy paste in the bottle containing the water.

Joseph Pearson was next on the stand; the *Norfolk Chronicle and Norwich Gazette* said that he 'detailed a great many hearsay stories, which could not be received in evidence'. Then he said that his niece Hannah Everett, who lived in Norwich, had been to his house and while she was 'looking over a bureau' she found a piece of paper marked 'poison' which contained white powder, and she threw it into the fire.

Was this the poison that ended up in the kettle? There was only one way to find out; the coroner adjourned the inquest and said that he planned to summon Hannah Everett to give evidence.

On 29 April 1847, the inquest was resumed at the Greyhound Inn, and Hannah Everett was called to testify. She deposed that she was the niece of the deceased and lived in Norwich. 'The day Aunt Elizabeth Everett was buried, I went to Tibenham. The following day, I was invited to Mr Pearson's house. I stayed there all day; I went there again on Monday and looked in the bureau to see if any of my aunt's things were in it. I found a little bottle in a drawer with white powder in it, labelled "Arsenic – poison". I burnt the powder and took charge of the bottle. Eliza Sage the servant came up and asked me what it was. I told her it was poison. I would have burned the bottle, too, but I thought it might fly up from the heat of fire, so I told Sage to bury it. She took it into the garden and I assume she buried it. I told her not to say anything. I told Uncle Pearson that I had burned poison but not about my order to bury the bottle.'

Why had she got rid of it?

'Mrs Reeve said on the day of the funeral that if any white powder was in the house, it would be better buried or burnt so no more harm could be done.'

Hannah Reeve was called to explain why she'd said that. 'On the day of the funeral, I said to Eliza Sage if any white powder was found in the house it might be better buried or burnt as it is dangerous for poison to be about. I asked her if she knew where her mistress keeps the poison; she said sometimes it was kept in the bureau.'

Lucy Ann Pearson, wife of John Pearson junior, deposed that on the Sunday when Mrs Pearson was ill she went to see her at about half past ten. 'I saw my aunt and Sage. Sage said my aunt was asleep and I must not wake her. I wanted to send for doctor but Sage said, "It's of no use. My mistress will not have the doctor."'

This seems odd, as Joseph Pearson claimed that he'd already sent for the doctor at that point.

'In a closet in my aunt's bedroom, I saw a basin with grease in it. I suppose it was poison. I left it there, but locked the door and gave Mr Pearson the key,' Lucy continued, 'My aunt appeared in a stupid state. I asked Sage about the poison and she said what was swept up was burnt.' More tellingly: 'When I went to the house on the morning of my aunt's death, the breakfast table was cleared. I can't say what happened to the water in kettle except for that put in the stone hot water bottle.'

So had Sage taken the opportunity to remove the kettle and rinse it? It was obvious to everyone else that in a case of suspected poisoning – as this clearly was – nothing should have been moved.

'I said to Sage, you have not behaved to your mistress as you ought to have done.' Lucy added. 'And Sage admitted it.'

James Warren was called back in; according to the *Norfolk Chronicle and Norwich Gazette* he had been 'under surveillance of the police, in order that the ends of justice might not be defeated'. Clearly the last couple of days had been good for his memory, because he said he remembered, 'Sage and my mistress had a few words on the Friday before her death, about weeding the flower garden. Eliza said the next night she had never seen such an old woman in her life.' So clearly things weren't as rosy between Sage and Mrs Pearson as Sage had deposed.

Warren added, 'Five weeks after Michaelmas, Sage called our mistress bad names and said "she would stive her old eyes".' In other words, Sage wanted to stifle or suffocate her mistress. The row obviously wasn't a one off, because, 'Last Christmas she aggravated Mrs Pearson to such an extent she was desired to pack up her things and go about her business.'

The situation had been smoothed over, but maybe the row about the weeding had been the last straw for Eliza Sage, and she'd just snapped and tipped the arsenic powder into the tea kettle, knowing that Mr Pearson would be drinking beer for breakfast and Warren would be drinking milk, so the only one to have tea would be the one she wanted to suffocate… with arsenic.

'Under surveillance' didn't necessarily mean in custody', because Warren's next statement implied that he'd still been living and working at the Pearson house. 'On the Saturday after the jury last met, she said to me, while I was washing in the back-house and getting ready for supper, "Don't you think I could make those gentlemen [the jury] believe a lie – if I was to tell them that you poisoned your mistress, and swear to it, would they not believe me?" I told her I did not know.'

So was Sage suggesting she would pin the blame on her fellow servant?

'She said, "If you were to swear I did it, don't you think they would believe you?"'

Probably not, because he'd already tried their patience by 'running on'.

She was clearly worried about the rumours in the village, because she complained to Warren that Mrs Reeve had been saying Sage knew where the poison was kept and it was a story: 'How could I tell her when I did not know where it was?'

The following Saturday, she told Warren it would be Hannah Everett's fault if she went to prison. 'She told me to bury the bottle and say nothing about it.' She also thought she'd be found guilty, because she said to Warren, 'I dare say I shall have to be hung,' and added, 'If I am hung, it will be for a good job, and I shall be one of the worst out of the parish.' Sage told Warren she knew he thought she did it, but he could have done it just as easily.

Rhoda Moore, Mr Pearson's housekeeper, testified next. She said that on the Saturday after the second day's proceedings, Sage told her, 'I have done such a thing on that day that I had not done before in my life.'

Did she mean that she'd poisoned Mrs Pearson?

Possibly not because she added that she couldn't tell because she had promised not to. So what she meant was that she'd buried the bottle. When the bottle was found, she admitted she put it there 'but only because Hannah Everett told me to', In Mrs Moore's view, Sage 'seemed to greatly regret the loss of her mistress'. Sage was also worried about what would happen to her: 'She said people reckoned she'd be sent to Wymondham Bridewell.'

And there wasn't much love lost between Sage and Warren; Mrs Moore didn't think they were friendly at all. 'The girl was of an aggravating temper and they quarrelled frequently.'

Other villages testified that Sage wasn't happy in the Pearson household. Lucy Sheldrake, said, 'I had heard Sage find fault with her mistress, who was always snubbing her, Sage said she would rather live in the workhouse than with her.' Pretty strong stuff: because by 1847 life in the workhouse was grim. Far from being 'pauper palaces', they were places where food was sparse, hours were long, and families were kept segregated.

Mrs Mary Lant and Mrs Ann Robinson both testified that Mrs Pearson had 'told them about her bad servant girl but didn't seem afraid the girl would do her a mischief'.

Interestingly, constable Frederick Bloomfield testified that he'd found the glass phial – and that Hannah Everett showed him where it was buried. Considering that Hannah had claimed earlier she just 'assumed' that Sage buried the bottle, and that Hannah had been the one to find the poison… did Hannah know more about the situation than she was letting on?

The inquiry was adjourned again.

Finally, the inquest was resumed at the Greyhound on 13 May. Mr Pilgrim, the coroner, said he doubted that any additional evidence would fix guilt on a single party. The final verdict was that Mary Pearson and Elizabeth Everett 'died from the effects of arsenic wilfully administered by some person or persons unknown'. Sage, Warren and Hannah Everett were the most likely suspects: but the proof just wasn't enough to convict any of them.

A Pennyworth of Rhubarb:
AUGUSTUS WORTS, 1850

The case of Augustus Worts is a rarity among the Norfolk poisons: rather than being a person wanting rid themselves of a spouse or child, or someone wanting to cash in on various people's life insurance, Augustus Worts was a professional accused of negligence leading to death by poison. The wrong drug was prescribed.

But there was a question over who made the mistake – the chemist's assistant or the girl who asked for the remedy?

It was all to do with a pennyworth of rhubarb. Rhubarb had hit the headlines three years before in the next-door county, Suffolk, when 18-year-old Catherine Foster was hanged for killing her husband by administering arsenic in a dumpling, a week after they'd got married. She'd seen the doctor in Melford and asked him for some medicine for John Foster, who had a 'bowel complaint'. Dr Robert Jones gave her two powders he'd mixed himself, of mercury (itself a poison) mixed with chalk and rhubarb; but when he called to see the patient he found Foster dead. When the stomach contents were analysed at the post mortem, Jones was off the hook: neither the mercury nor the rhubarb was responsible, because a large quantity of arsenic was present.

The case was reported in the *Bury and Norwich Post*, so it's entirely possible that Augustus Worts or his employer, the chemist Mr Smith of Magdalen Street, had read the report of the trial. And it's also possible that the Foster case made the chemists and druggists that much more aware that the drugs they prescribed could be used in an attempt to cover up murder, so they needed to take more care with their prescriptions.

But in March 1850, the murder of William Dix was clearly an accident rather than deliberate. Augustus Worts was asked for something for a 'bowel complaint', and the drug he gave caused William Dix to die. Did Augustus Worts give the drug he was asked for, or did he give the wrong one by mistake?

On 4 April 1850, Worts was indicted for manslaughter, charged with having administered a poisonous drug to William Dix, in consequence of which he died.

Thirteen-year-old Hannah Barker, apprentice to the dressmaker Elizabeth Mills of Magdalen Street, gave her version of events. 'William Dix lived next door. His wife came into my mistress's house on 12 March just before nine in the morning.' Mrs Dix was worried about her husband's condition and wanted some medicine for him. Hannah, as the apprentice, was used to running errands, and was duly despatched to the local chemist's to get something. 'She gave me a penny and I went to Mr Smith's in Magdalen Street.' Smith's the chemist was a family business that had been trading there for at least twenty years; Augustus Worts was the assistant. 'I saw Augustus Worts behind the counter, and said, "If you please, sir, I am come for a pennyworth of rhubarb for an old gentlemen troubled with the bowel complaint." He asked if it was to relieve the old man.'

A 'bowel complaint' usually meant constipation, and rhubarb was the most common remedy given to relieve the problem. However, Augustus clearly wanted to make sure that the girl was asking for the right thing; if the old gentleman was suffering from diarrhoea rather than constipation, rhubarb would make things worse and the chemist would be more likely to prescribe some kind of chalk mixture instead. Or the chemist might give a small dose of opium, which would act as a painkiller as well as a binding agent.

Hannah replied that she didn't know.

This is really where Augustus should have checked. (In fact, during his own statement, Augustus claimed that Hannah didn't ask for rhubarb: he said she asked for opium.)

According to Hannah, Augustus then gave her a pill box out of a drawer. 'I didn't see him put anything in it. Nothing was written on it.'

In Norwich at that time, opium was always dispensed in unmarked boxes.

As to the question of what she'd asked for, Hannah claimed that a blind boy had been in the shop at the time and overheard her conversation with Worts. She didn't know who he was, but she was sure that he would corroborate her story.

Elizabeth Mills, Hannah's employer, told the jury what happened next. 'I sent Hannah for a pennyworth of rhubarb. She came back with a box. I gave it to Mrs Dix, who opened it and saw something in the box.'

Lucy Dix, the widow of William Dix, took up the story. 'On 12 March Mrs Mills gave me box. I made the contents into three pills and gave them to my husband. When he fell asleep he wouldn't wake up again.'

With opium poisoning, the victim becomes drowsy; within a few hours, respiratory failure occurs. No details of Dix's symptoms were given at the inquest, but his skin would have felt cool and clammy to the touch, there would have been signs of cyanosis (blueness) around the mouth and nose and flushed cheeks, his pupils would have been contracted, his breathing would have become slower and noisier as his muscles relaxed, and his pulse would have weakened and gradually slowed down until it finally stopped.

Lucy Dix panicked and went next door to Elizabeth Mills. Elizabeth confirmed it: 'Mrs Dix came to me again and I said she should get the doctor.'

W. B. Francis, the local surgeon, came out to see Mr Dix at 12 o'clock. 'Augustus Worts told me the deceased took 30 grains of opium.' This is the equivalent of nearly two grams (one grain weighs about 65mg). Though Mr Francis wouldn't have had to be told that Mr Dix had take opium, as it had a very characteristic scent.

'We used a stomach pump and brought it up,' Francis continued, 'but the man died.' Lucy added that Mr Dix had 'lasted about twelve hours'.

It's hardly surprising that poor William didn't survive; a fatal dose is between three and five grains and he had been given enough to kill at least six people. 'The cause of death,' said Francis, 'was opium.'

Opium wasn't commonly used as a murderer's weapon in the nineteenth century; it was, however, the most common cause of accidental and suicidal poisoning.

'I've not seen opium before,' Mrs Dix said. 'I've only seen root of rhubarb that the Jews carry about.' In folk medicine, wearing the root of rhubarb on a string round your neck is supposed to prevent stomach aches. Clearly Lucy Dix thought that she was giving her husband rhubarb; there was no question that she was trying to get rid of her husband.

The jury at the inquest decided that Augustus gave Hannah opium, not rhubarb, by mistake.

Augustus knew that if he was found guilty of giving Hannah the wrong substance, he could be hanged for murder. According to the *Norwich Mercury*, he didn't wait for the verdict of the inquest – he absconded. However, his lawyer assured the coroner that Augustus would be there for the trial on 6 April.

In the meantime, policeman Richard Bungay found William Everett, a blind boy who worked at the Hospital for the Blind in Magdalen Street and who had been at the chemist's shop when Hannah asked for the medication.

The evidence at the trial was much the same as that given at the inquest – apart from William Everett's. 'I heard her ask for opium and the young man said that was not opening but binding.'

Mr Power, the defence lawyer, said that Hannah's statement was unreliable: she claimed that she'd asked for rhubarb but two people thought that she'd asked for opium. He added that Augustus Worts gave opium to her but not carelessly – he'd checked it with her first.

William Everett added that opium 'was a drug very much used in this city'. His evidence was corroborated by another witness, the chemist John Woolner from St Andrew's Hall Plain, who said, 'Opium is largely taken in Norwich as a stimulant, the same as drinking a dram.'

Mr Power told the jury that it was evident if thirteen-year-old Hannah had made a mistake and caused William Dix to die, she would be frightened and would want to conceal the mistake – which was why she'd insisted that she'd asked for rhubarb. He pointed out that if William Everett had been called to give evidence at the inquest, the case would not have come this far (i.e. to trial).

In his summing up, the judge explained to the jury that if they believed Augustus Worts had caused the death of William Dix by negligence or carelessness, they should return a verdict of guilty. If they believed that he made a mistake or the girl asked for opium (or Augustus *thought* she did), they should acquit him.

The jury found Augustus Worts not guilty.

The judge added that there was a 'degree of neglect involved in articles of this kind not being labelled poison'. The defence said that if the word 'poison' was put on the box, it would stop people buying something that was largely used as a stimulant. However, Mr Power said that the chemists in the city had agreed to put the word 'opium' on any boxes of the drug they sold from that date on.

Incidentally, it wasn't until the Poisons and Pharmacy Act of 1868 that it became illegal to sell drugs such as opium without a licence. Before then, opium-based products such as Godfrey's

Example of a typical poison bottle.

113

Cordial (a 'soother' for crying babies), Dover's Powders (a cure for gout) and laudanum (a tincture of opium in wine) were sold in pubs, grocers' shops and other non-pharmaceutical outlets. The use of opium (and its derivative, morphine) was restricted further by the Dangerous Drugs Act of 1920, which made it illegal to import or export opium, and the Regulations of 1921 which made it illegal to produce, prescribe or supply certain drugs (including opium) unless you were a medical practitioner, dentist or vet, or had a special licence granted by the Secretary of State (i.e. the Home Secretary).

The Specked Cake:
WILLIAM AND SUSANNAH DAVEY, 1869

'Inheritance powder' came to the fore again in the case of William and Susannah Davey. This time, the poison used wasn't arsenic: it was 'white precipitate', better known as precipitate of mercury.

Mercury was known to be a toxin – in Victorian times, 'mad hatters' cured the fur trims of hats with mercury, inhaled the vapours and developed hallucinations, personality changes and dementia. Acute mercury poisoning causes stomach pains, diarrhoea, vomiting and haemorrhage; more long-term poisoning also causes soreness of the tongue, gums and tissues lining the mouth.

On 12 August 1869, thirty-two-year-old William George Davey and his wife Susannah were indicted for administering poison to John Mayes Davey, William's elder brother, with intent to murder or to endanger his life.

Thirty-three-year-old John survived to tell the tale. He explained that he and and William were originally partners in a bakery in Pakefield, Suffolk; however, there wasn't enough business to support both of them. 'I dissolved the partnership on good terms with my brother,' he said, 'and went to be a journeyman miller in Swaffham.' He lodged with a tailor called Robert Harvey.

John went to London early in May 1869; his mother had died two years previously, intestate. 'The Accountant General gave me £43,' he explained – this was because John, as the elder brother, was the administrator of his mother's estate. 'I paid the solicitor and had £39 left.' When he left London, John went to see William in Pakefield and stayed there for a few days. 'I gave my brother £10, which was more than was due to him from the intestate will. My brother and his wife said nothing but looked disappointed.' They were dissatisfied, he felt; though they had no cause. 'After I paid my brother £10, I paid most of the rest of the money out for my mother's debts.' If anything, John was the brother who'd come off worst.

The prosecution alleged that William and Susanna's chief motive was the fact that they were John's heirs, so if he died they'd get all his property. John was single and had been left some money by an uncle, so his estate would be worth £80 (about £5,100 in today's money).

John explained that he earned eleven shillings a week. He added that he had been on good terms with his brother for his entire life – and even gave his brother a character witness! 'My brother has been the overseer of the parish,' said John: hardly the kind of job that would be given to someone of a dubious moral character.

His brother and sister-in-law had lodgers, Mr and Mrs Halliday, although they didn't take meals together. 'On Sunday 9 May we had dinner with plum pudding. Susannah said she had made me a plum pudding to take home, and some cake,' John said, adding, 'I like cakes and he doesn't.'

John left Pakefield on 11 May and returned to Swaffham. Before he left, they talked about the possibility of William coming to visit him. Then William gave him a hamper containing six cakes, which John described: 'Two of the cakes had been baked in half-quartern tins.' Bread made in a half-quartern tin would weigh about 2 lbs or just under a kilogram, so they were fairly substantial cakes. 'The smaller ones were four inches long and 2 inches broad; all of them were brownish.'

Although it was the first time Susannah had ever offered to make him cakes, John wasn't in the least suspicious, and ate some of the cakes at teatime when he got home. He caused some hilarity in the court when he

Swaffham where John Davey survived the poisoned cakes.

116

admitted that he hadn't actually shared any of them with his landlord's children.

'You must *really* like cake,' one of the jurors said.

William came to visit John on 14 May; that evening, they had tea together, but William refused to eat any of the cakes. John wasn't that surprised, as his brother had never been that keen on cake.

On 23 May, at around 5 p.m., John had another of the cakes for tea. He ate half of it, but then noticed 'specks of white as big as grains of rice' in the cake. The first mouthful tasted old (hardly surprising, as the cake had been made nearly two weeks before) and a bit salty. He spat out the third mouthful and didn't eat any more.

Tellingly, the cake he'd spat out was eaten by his landlord's hens – and the birds quickly became ill.

About a quarter of an hour after tea, John felt sick and 'was purged'. There was a salty taste in his mouth, and it felt 'hot'. He went to chapel, came home again at about 8 p.m. and was seized with violent vomiting and purging. Scarily, the vomit was blood red. He was forced to get out of bed in the middle of the night, 'violently sick and purging'; the attack lasted until midday and was so severe that his life was in danger.

Robert Harvey, his landlord, testified that the hens were ill and he saw the vomit in the basin. He sent for Mr Marriott, the village doctor. Robert's son John said that he'd offered some of the specked cake to the cat, which refused to eat it, so he thought it must be poisoned and told his father. Robert preserved the vomit and the spat-out cake for the doctor to run tests.

John was given medical treatment and recovered, but testified that he was very weak for a long time, and the roof of his mouth was still very sore.

Mr Marriott, the doctor at Swaffham, and Professor Taylor of Guy's Hospital analysed the remaining cake, the uneaten cake and what John had vomited. 'It was clearly a metallic irritant poison,' said the doctor. 'I thought it was arsenic, but it turned out to be white precipitate, a preparation of mercury.' The tests showed that there was white precipitate in the remaining cake and the contents of the stomach, but nothing in the uneaten cake.

Professor Taylor told the jury that he found no baking powder in the cake; this is unusual, as cakes in the nineteenth century were made with plain flour and baking powder. He explained that baking powder is a compound of tartaric acid and carbonate of soda, 'whose nature is destroyed as soon as it is used; the water decomposes it and gives porosity to bread'. White precipitate, on the other hand, was usually mixed with lard and used externally as an ointment to cure ringworm in dogs, and in a powdered form to kill insects. It was also used in preparation of chignons and false hair. It wasn't actually classed as a poison, so there were no restrictions on its sale, though the professor had campaigned to have it included in the Poisons Act.

'It's a peculiar poison,' he said. 'It produces a most violent action of the stomach, and thus persons have a greater chance of recovery by its being thrown off.' He said that it was comparatively rare. 'I have collected fourteen cases, out of which two were fatal; one was at Chelmsford twenty years ago.' (However, he may have been muddled here. The poisoning cases in Essex twenty years before were those of Sarah Chesham – acquitted of poisoning her children in 1845–7, but finally hanged for the murder of her husband Richard in 1851 – and that of Mary May, hanged for the murder of her half-brother William Constable in 1848; both women used arsenic.)

Superintendent George Lambley deposed that on Monday 24 May he saw the vomit in the basin, found out who made the cakes, and travelled to Pakefield. On Thursday 27 May he apprehended Susannah and told her he had a warrant to arrest her for poisoning with intent to murder her brother-in-law by cakes. 'She made a rush for the back of shop and said she wanted to see her husband,' he said. He refused, and left her in the custody of PC Nurse. 'Then I went to arrest William Davey. I tapped him on the shoulder and he turned round and said, "You've come to see me about my brother," before I even had a chance to mention it.' It's possible that William believed the only reason the police would visit him was if something had happened to his brother, as he was John's next of kin. On the other hand, it could be that he had a guilty conscience.

'He asked if his brother was dead,' Lambley continued. 'I said no. I searched the house, and Susannah said, "After this I'll cut him, I'll have no more of him."' This seems a very odd thing to say; was she aware that William had poisoned the cake? Had the poisoning been William's idea but she'd been the one to go through with it?

The defence lawyer, Mr Metcalfe, argued that William and Susannah had mistaken the white powder for baking powder, 'which it much resembled'. He said that the mistake had probably been made in the grocer's shop in the first place, as baking powder was widely sold in penny packets. He also felt there was no motive, as William and

Susannah had never even tried to borrow money from John. As for putting poison in the cake: although baking power 'diffused in dough', a white precipitate would sink in just one place. That was why only one cake was poisoned; and because the Daveys would expect John to offer some of the cake to the landlady's children, they wouldn't have poisoned the cake because they wouldn't have wanted to kill the children.

Justice Byles agreed that it would be difficult to say which of the Daveys had put the poison intentionally in the cake. The wife had made the cakes, but the husband might have put the poison in the dough after it had been put in the tins. His view was that William was more guilty than his wife.

The problem was, as usual, lack of evidence. There were no forensic tests to support the investigation. And the jury could do only one thing: they acquitted the Daveys.

A Melancholy Turn of Mind:
MARY ANN LANGFORD, 1869

The case of Mary Ann Langford is terribly sad – a case where a woman's circumstances drove her beyond the point of desperation, so she ended up using strychnine on her husband and daughter, before trying to use it on herself.

Mary Ann was indicted for the murder of her daughter Charlotte Langford at King's Lynn. The little girl was four months old; she died at 6 p.m. on 26 April. Dr Lowe, the family's medical adviser, did the post mortem. He thought that the child's organs were all healthy and he couldn't see a natural cause for her death, so he suspected the cause was poison. He sent the organs to Dr Letheby (described in the *Norfolk Chronicle and Norwich Gazette* as an 'analytical chemist and professor of the London Hospital'), who discovered the presence of strychnine.

The prosecution's lawyer explained that Mary Ann had married Alfred Langford, a chemist and druggist in Norwich, around sixteen years ago. They moved to King's Lynn, and Alfred had been ill for the

Norfolk Street, King's Lynn where the Langfords' pharmacy once stood.

last two years, and bedridden since April. Mary Ann looked after him well and had an excellent character; there appeared to be no motive for her to murder her husband or child. But, as the lawyer pointed out, Mary Ann had a large family of young children; her husband had been very ill for the previous two years, and needed a lot of looking after; and on top of this workload she had to attend to the family business, which was going rapidly downhill.

It was hardly surprising that the strain became too much for her. She was 'of a melancholy turn of mind', so she snapped and was guilty of murder, 'this most unnatural act'.

At this point of the trial, Mary Ann burst into tears; the court was humane enough to give her a seat.

Susan Langford, Mary Ann's mother-in-law, was the first to give evidence. She testified that she lived at King's Lynn and was the wife of the chemist William Langford; she was also the mother of the late Albert Langford. 'On 26 April, I was sent for to go to my son's at Norfolk Street. I got there at 8.15 and asked if Albert was worse this morning. Mary Ann said he'd got out of bed and she had trouble getting him back. The baby was downstairs. I saw it was very ill and convulsed. One of the little girls was nursing it on her lap,' Susan continued, 'but Mary Ann said she had not sent for the doctor.'

George Liker, Albert's apprentice, took up the story. 'I came in at seven that morning. Dr Lowe came at quarter past nine, asked me for an emetic and sent me for Dr Archer. Mary Ann tried to get out through the railway passage –' this was a passage leading from the house to the street, which could be used by people in the shop as well '– but I wouldn't let her because she was in a wild, excited state.'

Ann Beavis, Albert's aunt, told the court that she was a widow who lived with her sister, Mrs William Langford (i.e. Susan). 'On 26 April at 8.30 I went to Mary Ann's bedroom. I didn't see Charlotte there. I saw it at 9.30 in its cradle. It was in convulsions all day.'

Elizabeth Sayers, a dressmaker from Chapel Street, King's Lynn, was also at the Langford house that day. 'I have known Mary Ann a long time. The baby looked ill, so I nursed it. It kept convulsing, and its hands twitched. I gave the child milk and water out of a teacup, but the child didn't have the strength to swallow.'

Ann Beavis said that Dr Archer administered an emetic to the baby.

'Then it vomited about half a teaspoon of yellow froth,' Elizabeth Sayers added. 'It died at around 6 p.m.'

Ann Beavis told the jury that Charlotte wasn't the only one in convulsions that day. 'Dr Lowe took something from Mary Ann's dress pocket. She was in strong convulsions and said, "Forgive me."'

Ann also shed light on the Langfords' circumstances. 'My nephew has been ill in mind and body. They have seven children; the eldest son is fourteen or fifteen, and the eldest daughter is thirteen. They have no servant.'

A household of nine would mean a great deal of domestic work, but that wasn't all Mary Ann had to contend with. Elizabeth explained to the court, 'Mary Ann was low after her confinement. She was an affectionate mother and an attentive wife, but her husband needed much attendance. He couldn't do anything.' So his share of the work – running the chemist's shop – fell to Mary Ann. And on top of that, she had to look after him. He clearly wasn't an easy patient; according to Elizabeth, 'He gets out of bed and wanders around with no clothes on.'

Liker testified that Mary Ann assisted in the shop, though Frederick George Miles explained what her role was: 'Mary Ann never dispensed; she only sold tobacco and dealt with the takings.'

Dr Lowe testified that when he was called to see Albert, he noticed the patient was convulsed. 'I asked Mary Ann how long, and she admitted, "Doctor, I could not bear it any longer. I have poisoned myself."' He asked, 'What about your husband?' She said yes, she'd poisoned him too. The convulsions made him suspect exactly what she'd used: 'With strychnine?' he asked. Mary Ann said yes – and went into convulsions.

Lowe gave them both an emetic, then saw that Charlotte, too, was convulsing. 'It could be due to strychnine or it could just be childhood convulsions,' he thought. Somebody – it wasn't clear who – gave him Mary Ann's gown. 'There was a crystalline substance in the pocket. I put it in a paper and sealed it and kept it until I sent it to Dr Letheby.'

He didn't have time to make notes until later that evening, and admitted that although he'd been examined five times by the coroner he'd only recently re-read his notes. 'Albert lived until 6 May, and I can't say he died from strychnine,' he added. 'The danger is over when the convulsions stop. Strychnine may irritate the membranes of the stomach, alimentary canal and brain; it may kill in one and a half to two hours. If you survive for three to four hours, you are likely to recover.' He told the court, 'A fraction of a grain will kill an adult and a very small fraction will kill a child.'

Strychnine was definitely in the shop. 'We keep poisons, including strychnine, in a drawer,' Liker said.

Albert Langford was taking medication prescribed by Dr Lowe; as Lowe explained to the court, he prescribed *nux vomica* for Albert's condition. And *nux vomica* contained strychnine. 'About two or three per cent,' Lowe said. Though someone wasn't likely to take it by mistake, as 'it has a bitter taste.' Lowe did however admit that if it was wrongly made up, it could kill. And Albert – being a chemist by trade – liked to mix up his own medication.

Dr Edward Archer did the post mortem on the baby. He was too ill to attend court, but gave a statement saying that the convulsions weren't necessarily caused by strychnine; they could be from tetanus, 'which is likely to arise in a child from a trifling cause such as a cold.' But if it was strychnine, it didn't mean that Mary Ann had actually given it to the child. It could be that Mary Ann had tried to poison herself and some of the poison had already gone through to her breast milk: 'The child might imbibe poison from its mother's breast.' But he added that crystalline strychnine (which was the sort found in Mary Ann's dress) was not readily absorbed.

Dr Letheby examined the baby's organs and found traces of strychnine in the liver. His tests there were entirely practical; he tasted it himself and found it bitter, and then gave it to a frog, which died. The rest of his tests, on the contents of the baby's stomach were chemically based, using 'evaporation and application of peroxide of manganese'. 'The baby's stomach had farinaceous matter and milk in it,' said Letheby, and the tests he did 'produced the red and violet colours typical of strychnia': so strychnine was definitely present in the milk and 'farinaceous mater'.

Dr Taylor, professor of chemistry at Guy's Hospital (who had also performed tests in the Davey case, earlier that year) said that the symptoms exhibited by the baby were those of strychnine.

The prosecution's stance was that 'the prisoner is guilty of this unnatural act'.

The defence refuted this. There was no motive. Yes, her husband was ill – dying, even – and she had seven children, but she'd cared for them all for two years. 'She is not likely to turn from a good mother and wife overnight and murder those she loved and cherished,' they pointed out.

As for the business: 'there is no proof of poverty.' The prosecution pointed out that for financial reasons, she wouldn't murder her husband, because 'she couldn't carry on the business in his name if he died, and she would be thrown on the world.'

If – and it was a big if – Mary Ann had poisoned her baby, the prosecution thought it must have been 'in a moment when she was deserted by her senses and incapable of judging the nature of the act'.

Plus Charlotte took nine hours to die: it had never been known for a child to take nine hours to die from strychnine poisoning. In the post mortem, there was no proof of congestion or irritation of the membranes, as a scientist would expect from strychnine poisoning.

And, most crucially, there was no proof that Mary Ann had administered the poison. It could have been Albert, who liked to mix his own medicines but was ill and had miscalculated the dosages; or it could be that Mary Ann had found him with the poison, feared that he was going to do himself an injury, and taken the poison from him, putting it in her pocket out of his way. Afterwards, there could accidentally have been a minute amount on her hanky or fingers, which somehow got into the baby's mouth.

What about Mary Ann's statements to Dr Lowe and Dr Archer, that she had poisoned her husband and herself and asked them to forgive her? The defence lawyer said that the prosecution couldn't rely on those statements, because at the time Mary Ann was extremely distressed and 'was not conscious all the time of what she was doing'.

The judge said it was plain that Mary Ann had no intention or ill feeling towards her child or her husband, but if she had been prompted to relieve her troubles in a criminal way, then she was guilty of murder. If she had poisoned herself and communicated the strychnine to the child through her breast milk, , then she was guilty of murder. He felt that the evidence showed that the child had died from poison, but how had it been administered and by whom?

The jury retired. After fifteen minutes, their verdict was that Mary Ann was not guilty of poisoning her daughter.

Mary Ann was then charged with the murder of Albert Francis Longford. She pleaded not guilty. The judge said that if she had used strychnine, Albert would have died sooner: there was no evidence of her guilt. Again, the jury gave a 'not guilty' verdict and discharged her.

Guilty of Misdemeanour:
HANNAH WILLIMOTT, 1870

Hannah Willimott's case is unusual because of the poison involved: phosphorus. Phosphorus was used in the early nineteenth century as part of a nerve tonic, though the medicines contained too small a dose to poison anyone. Matches were another source of phosphorus; children sucking match-heads could be accidentally poisoned, but an adult would have to consume 100mg (roughly the amount contained in an entire box of matches) for the dose to be fatal. The most common source of phosphorus in Victorian times was rat poison, which was thought to be safer than arsenic; it consisted of bran mixed with black treacle and about 2% phosphorus. The poison was sold in a small, shallow tin which was left opened for rats to find it; although phosphorus smells and tastes strongly of garlic, that didn't bother the rats.

Phosphorus poisoning causes dehydration, making the victims extremely thirsty; they will also suffer from convulsions and diarrhoea. A post mortem will reveal an inflamed stomach, plus enlarged and yellowish kidneys and liver; however, this can mimic the symptoms of liver disease. There is one big giveaway with phosphorus, however: it glows in the dark. One of the tests for the presence of phosphorus, Mitscherlich's test, involved heating a sample with acid in total darkness (rather dangerous!) and the vapour given off would glow. Another test, Scherer's test, also heated the sample with acid, but a piece of filter paper soaked in silver nitrate was placed across the top of the flask. If it turned black, phosphorus was present.

Murder by phosphorus wasn't common in England in the nineteenth century. The main reason was that the taste and smell of the poison wasn't easy to disguise (unlike that of arsenic) so the victim was unlikely to consume food or drink poisoned by phosphorus. There was a case in Bodmin in 1839 where a man decided that his three-year-old illegitimate granddaughter was a burden; in a horrible twist, he persuaded his daughter to buy the rat poison used to kill the child. Originally he asked for arsenic, but the chemist refused to sell it and sent Grace Beard home with some phosphorus-based paste instead. A neighbour saw the little girl eating a crust of bread 'spread with something dark'; and John Beard's behaviour was suspicious, to say the least. However, the jury acquitted him – in part because the main witness for the prosecution was the little girl's mother, who had also been charged with the murder but had been aquitted.

On 23 December 1870, sixteen-year old Hannah Willimott was charged with administering 'vermin killer' to the eight-day-old baby of Peter Woodcock at Hainford, with intent to murder it.

Woodcock, a fowl dealer, testified that until recently he had a wife and four children. He'd employed Hannah since Michaelmas (about three months) to look after the children. 'She always seemed kind and the children were fond of her.'

Then, on 2 December, Mrs Woodcock had a baby boy.

Woodcock explained that he had bought some vermin killer from Messrs Andrews Bros, the chemist at St George, because 'the house was troubled with rats'. He explained that the mixture was in an earthern jar; there were directions on the jar for the use of the poison, and it said 'keep away from children'. He put the poison on a baulk in his wash house, although he didn't actually use it. He had, however, used poison in Hannah's presence before; he'd spread it on bread then put it on a beam, which happened to be within her reach.

Martha Loveday was the nurse who'd attended Mrs Woodcock during the pregnancy and birth. 'The girl had no business with the baby as I was there for that,' she said. On 10 December, Mrs Loveday went to Mrs Woodcock's room to look after the baby, and saw Hannah by the bed next to the baby. 'Why are you there?' she asked.

Hannah said, 'I heard the child crying.'

Mrs Loveday clearly didn't believe her. 'If you had heard it, I should have heard it too, and even if you had heard it, what business had you to come up?' Harsh – but there was a very rigid social hierarchy in Victorian times, and Mrs Loveday clearly intended to make sure that Hannah knew her place. 'You should have come to me and told me.'

Mrs Loveday took the baby down to Mrs Woodcock, who made a remark about something being on the child's face. Mrs Loveday took a rag and wiped it; she saw some mixture on the material but didn't know what it was. 'I saw something like steam or smoke coming from the baby's mouth,' she said. That would have been phosphorus vapour. 'Then I saw blue stuff on the baby's tongue.'

Clearly Hannah had done something she shouldn't have done. And

Mrs Loveday tackled Hannah that evening, when they both went to see shopkeeper Mr Roberts. 'I asked her why she did such a wicked thing.'

Hannah's response: 'If there had been only four children and no additions to the family, I could have done for the family.' Clearly she felt unable to cope with looking after five children. 'Oh, Mrs Loveday, I wish I had never done it,' she said.

Mrs Loveday gave her rather short shrift. 'I told her it was too late now.'

Hannah confessed that she had put her finger in the poison pot, then into the baby's mouth. She had to 'put [her] foot in the brickwork of the wall to reach the pot'.

Mr Roberts testified next. He said that Martha Loveday had brought him a piece of calico stained blue, which she had used to wipe the baby's mouth. He thought the mixture looked like phosphorus, and gave the cloth to Detective Hudson on Friday 13 December. The same day, William Fields, a labourer in the employ of Mr Woodcock, took the jar from the baulk in the wash house and gave it to the detective.

Detective Hudson said that both the rag and pot smelled like Lucifer matches (i.e. contained phosphorus). He arrested Hannah at her sister's house; he cautioned her and told her he was police officer, at which point she began to cry and admitted what she'd done.

He gave the cloth and pot to chemist Francis Sutton for analysis. Sutton said that the rag contained phosphorus, and the jar contained a mixture of phosphorus, malt flour and fat. 'It is a slow-acting poison but causes death. A piece the size of a pea would kill an eight-day-old baby; a tenth of a grain [about 6.5g], if swallowed, would kill.'

Happily, the little boy lived. Hannah was committed to the Assizes.

The judge said that Willimott had no motive, unless she thought the child would give her additional trouble or work, although the baby 'didn't seem more restless or crying than a normal baby'. Hannah admitted putting it in the baby's mouth; the judge said the jury needed to think whether she administered it knowing it was poison, and what her motive was.

The jury found her guilty of administering poison with intent to injure the child, but recommended mercy on ground of her youth and previous good character. She was sentenced to six months' imprisonment with hard labour.

A year later, eighteen-year-old Charlotte Fisher was indicted for attempting to administer 'vermin poison' to her employers, Benjamin and Sarah Barnard, in Great Ellingham; after a row, Fisher was given notice to leave. That afternoon she took the tea-things into the dining room, but when Sarah Barnard poured hot water into the teapot she noticed the water was black and smelled awful. She made her servant put the water into a jar, which she gave to the chemist Mr Sutton; chemical analysis showed that the water contained enough phosphorus to kill. It was shown that Benjamin Barnard kept a pot of phosphorus paste lying around the house; although the jury found Fisher guilty (and she was sentenced to penal servitude for life), they also censured the Barnards 'for leaving so dangerous a poison as phosphorus within reach of so young a girl as the prisoner'.